How to
MAKE YOUR OWN
FISHING RODS

Mel Marshall

OUTDOOR LIFE BOOKS
New York

STACKPOLE BOOKS
Harrisburg, Pennsylvania

Published by

Outdoor Life Books
Times Mirror Magazines, Inc.
380 Madison Avenue
New York, NY 10017

Distributed to the trade by

Stackpole Books
Box 1831
Cameron & Kelker Streets
Harrisburg, PA 17105

Library of Congress Catalog Card Number: 78-62945
ISBN: 0-943822-12-2

Ninth Printing, 1983

Manufactured in the United States of America

Contents

Preface

This book may tell you more about building your own fishing rods than you really want to know. That's because it covers everything from simple cane poles for stillfishing to the sturdy regulation tackle rods used when trolling offshore for the saltwater giants. In between you'll encounter fly and spinning rods that will match any kind of fish or water, baitcasting rods, surf rods, boat and pier rods, specialty rods.

Assuming that you're a fisherman, you'll probably already be acquainted with most of the components described and the processes that are explained in such detail. This is even more likely to be the case if you've begun building rods as a hobby. Remember that there are novice fishermen who talk about "those little holes the line goes through" when describing a guide, and some who may even call a fishing rod a "pole." They're starting from square one, where all of us must begin, and need the basics you already know.

If you find yourself retracing familiar ground, be patient. That paragraph you're tempted to skip might contain an easier way of doing something, a component that will start you thinking about a fresh approach to rod design, or some small detail that will help you get more satisfaction from building rods that are yours alone, individual and unique.

Very large contributions to the text and pictures in this book have been made by a lot of people in the fishing tackle industry, who took the time and effort to provide me with details of manufacturing processes and product details. Though responsibility for the conclusions and opinions in the text is mine, and I don't always agree with some of the data I've received, the text would have been less complete without it.

Many thanks, then, to those who gave personal help: Gordon Allen, Bill Barlow, Ted Benson, Helen Blasky, Jim Butler, Al Carver, E. M. Elliott, George Hine, Bob Hipp, Fred Hooven, Bill Litwianik, Gary Loomis, Dave Myers, Bob Phillip, Don Rienzo, Bill Shedd, Jon Siversten, Tony Skilton, Milt Stevens, Mike Stoker, Dick Swann, Kevin Thompson, Vince Vella, Clare Zumpano.

For providing products discussed in the text and shown in the illustrations, I'm grateful to Allan Tackle Manufacturing Co., Axelson Fishing Tackle Manufacturing Co., Browning, California Tackle Co., Lew Childre & Sons, Featherweight Products, Fenwick, Gudebrod Bros. Silk Co., Lamiglas, Inc., Limit Manufacturing Co., Mildrum Manufacturing Co., Orvis Company, Plas/Steel Products, St. Croix Corporation, Scientific Anglers, Shakespeare Co., and Varmac Manufacturing Co.

There are others whose help lies far in the past. They're the men who guided me when I was beginning to learn the pleasures of rod making, who cheerfully corrected my mistakes and shared their knowledge of what was then an arcane craft practiced by only a few. My debt to them is great: E. C. "Pop" Powell, Charlie Kewell, Hugh McClung, Jack Cuthrell. All of them are now fishing in paradisiacal streams where every cast brings a strike and the sun never sets on clear, unpolluted waters.

MEL MARSHALL
Phillips, Texas

1

Fishing Rod Families

EVEN THOUGH THEY'RE inanimate and sexless, fishing rods breed prolifically. It's a rare angler who doesn't go to his rod storage closet or case and find twenty rods where only ten rested the last time he looked. He knows he hasn't bought any new rods lately, or been given any, but there they are. How their number can multiply without him being aware of it must be one of angling's greatest mysteries.

Since the first fishermen of antiquity learned that a springy rod could place a lure further and more accurately than a handline, and could also make playing and landing a fish a lot easier, the rod family has multiplied tremendously. Anglers who visit several different kinds of water and who seek a variety of fish have found that their days of sport are both more enjoyable and more productive when they indulge in a certain amount of rod specialization. It's always more fun to fish with a rod designed to do that particular kind of angling with superb efficiency.

A lot of fishermen have discovered, too, that building their own rods not only makes this specialization more economical, but allows them to experiment, to test their own theories of what a rod should be like in action and appearance. They've also found that there's a great deal of satisfaction in landing a fish with a rod they've built themselves.

For working purposes, all fishing rods can be divided into families and subfamilies. The major divisions, of course, are saltwater and freshwater rods, but just as in human families where cousins sometimes marry, relationships get a bit confused even between these two major divisions. Some rods function equally well when used in certain styles of fresh- and saltwater angling, but at least the freshwater-saltwater split gives us a place from which to start.

The next step is to put freshwater rods into four major groupings—there are several minor ones as well—depending on the style or manner of angling for which each group is designed. This is admittedly an imprecise way of classifying, but it's the one handed down to us by tradition and will have to serve until time changes our thinking habits. It lends itself to blurred spots, but these can be cleared up as we move along.

1

Simplest of all rods are those used in stillfishing. They are the only kind that should be called "poles," and are the direct descendants of the bare cane poles without any fittings with which the entire rod family began. Today, stillfishing poles are as commonly made of fiberglass as they are of the traditional cane or bamboo, and the fiberglass models often telescope, each section fitting inside another of slightly larger diameter. Such poles are usually extended with a flipping motion and might be referred to as "whipouts." Stillfishing poles are commonly from 10 to 14 feet long, and more and more are being fitted with a guide or two, sometimes a reel, less often a grip. They are used with lines just a little longer than the pole itself, and the lure or bait is flipped into the water rather than cast.

Next come baitcast/spincast rods, and this is one of the types where the division is somewhat blurred. Multiplying revolving-spool reels and closed-face spinning (or spincast) reels are used on these rods interchangeably. If there's a difference between a rod designed for a multiplying reel and one to be used with a spincast reel, it's so small as to be almost invisible. Baitcast rods are usually a few inches shorter, and spincast rods are often fitted with a slightly oversized butt or header guide. Offset grips with integral reel seats are generally fitted to such rods. The blades may be anywhere from 4 to 6 feet for baitcast rods, from 5 to $6^{1}/_{2}$ feet for spincast rods. On most of them, either the revolving spool reel or the spincast reel can be used interchangeably.

Spinning rods are designed specifically for use with open-faced fixed spool reels. They range in action from fast-tip to slow, in weight from ultralight to heavy, in length from $4^{1}/_{2}$ or 5 feet to 8 or 9 feet, and have straight handles. The handles on ultralight and light spinning rods often have all-cork grips with retaining rings to clamp the reel on. Heavier versions generally have a fixed reel seat between a butt grip and short foregrip.

Fly rods are the fourth general group. They run the gamut of weights from an ounce or so up to 10 or 12 ounces, lengths from 6 feet for fairy or flea rods up to 9 or even 10 feet for rods that are intended for steelhead fishing in big, fast rivers. The fly rod group also includes two-hand salmon rods that may go up to 14 feet in length. Actions vary from fast-tip rods, used in dry-fly fishing, to medium- and slow-tip rods in which the action extends all the way to the butt; these are used in wet-fly fishing.

Specialty rods include those designed for ice fishing, often called "jig rods" from the type of lure most often used with them; heavy-walled muskie rods, which are scaled-up versions of baitcast rods; popping rods, which are a stout spinning or baitcast rod; combination or convertible rods that can be jointed up to produce a passable spinning rod or fly rod; pack or trail rods that break down into four or more sections for easy portability; and the newest of all, maxi-rods, which are very long, very flexible rods designed to take big fish on extremely light lines.

As you can see, there are no precise specifications attached to any of these major freshwater families. This is one of the things that makes rod building such a challenging avocation for the fisherman. If you want to try new designs, new ideas, or simply to make rods best suited to your own height, strength, and style of angling, the only limits are your own skill, ingenuity, and imagination.

Saltwater groups aren't quite as numerous or diverse as those in the freshwater rod family. The traditional groupings are pier/boat, surf, and trolling rods; the saltwater fly rod is just a beefed-up freshwater fly rod and will be covered in the chapter devoted to rods of this kind.

Pier/boat rods are the workhorses of the saltwater family. They are medium-weight rods, usually 6 to 7 or 7½ feet long, with husky grips and reel seats. These rods are usually employed when fishing from a pier or jetty and may be called jetty rods; they are also used for bait fishing from a boat, and most of them are heavy enough to be used for light trolling.

Surf rods are enlarged spinning rods; some are designed to be used with spinning reels, others with free-spool revolving spool reels. They usually range in length from 9 to 11 feet and are capable of casting several ounces of weight plus a natural bait far out from shore.

Trolling rods are short, sturdy jobs with heavy-duty reel seats and roller guides and tops. They're also called "regulation tackle" rods, abbreviated as RT, and "game-fish" rods, which to me seems a misnomer, as all fishing rods, whether used in fresh or salt water, could properly be called "game-fish" rods. A trolling rod is usually classed by the weight of the line for which it is designed, and may be identified as a 12# or 20# or 30# up to a 180# rod. This identification is based on rules of the International Game Fish Association (IGFA), which governs and judges world record saltwater catches. We'll explore this in greater detail later on. The mechanics of rods and other tackle, whether freshwater or salt, are dictated by fishing common sense. There's not a great deal of virtue in hauling quarter-pound or half-pound panfish in with a 20-pound test line and a rod that has all the flexibility of a pool cue. Taken on an ultralight spinning rod or a fly rod, though, a panfish provides a lot of sport. At the other end of the scale, it's a waste of fishing hours to use ultralight tackle when fishing a weed-thick pond for black bass that might weigh 3 or 4 pounds—more, if you're lucky—and losing in the weeds almost every fish that strikes.

Giving the fish a chance to match its strength against tackle scaled to its size and habitat has come to be accepted by most fishermen as the criterion of sport fishing. As will be seen later, this doesn't mean giving an undue advantage to either the fish or the angler.

So, fishing rods are of many types, and each type has its place. The fisherman's problem in assembling his array of tackle is to match the gear he uses with the water and type of fish he's after. Assuming that you're a reasonably active angler, you already know this. Your problem is acquiring the number of rods you want without bankruptcy, especially during an era when the cost of everything keeps going up. Building your own rods is a very good solution, whether you're addicted to fishing with bait, lures, or flies. Fishing-tackle know-how and design have come a long way from the day when the angler's only choice was a simple, unaltered cane pole, or a willow branch cut from a tree at streamside.

Nobody really knows when the cane pole-willow branch age of fishing was superseded by the age of specialized rods; nobody really knows when fishermen started using rods instead of handlines. There are several theories that are supposed to explain how the rod was discovered, and I'm torn between two of them, both equally logical. One theory is that some prehistoric angler tied his handline to the branch of a brush or tree beside a stream, and when a fish gulped the bait this thoughtful primitive noticed how the springy limb held the fish hooked by bending and straightening, and with that as an example, went on to develop the rod by cutting off the limb and using it.

It's hard to ignore the second theory, though. This one surmises that rods evolved from the fish-spears used by ancient man. Most such spears had a barbed point—of shell or flint in the days before men learned to work metals—and this point was fitted into a slot at the spear's tip, held to it by a short length of thong. This theory also requires an observant, deductive angler who noticed that the longer the thong, the easier it was to play and tire a fish in which the spear's loose barb was embedded. Over the years, the thong became longer and the spear-shaft more flexible, until in time the fishing rod was born.

Either of these guesses seems about equally logical, but they are only two out of several other choices, so if you have a theory of your own, it could be equally valid. History simply doesn't record the date when the rod came into widespread use, or the area in which it evolved. Anglers using long rods made from water-reeds tied together are pictured in Egyptian tombs dated as far back as 3500 B.C.; these are the first known illustrations of fishing rods. The origin of the made-up or manufactured rod is fairly recent and well documented. Rods made by scraping long, straight hardwood limbs to a smooth taper are shown in woodcuts of the early 1600s and are described as early as the mid-1400s.

Somewhere during the 1500s, multi-strip made-up rods appeared. These were made of four strips of wood, the cross-section of each piece being an equilateral triangle tapered from butt to tip. When the strips were glued together lengthwise, a four-sided rod resulted. Though none of these is known to have survived for modern inspection, experts believe that hickory was the wood most often used. Later, these rods were extended by gluing up several short tapered strips and binding the spots where they butted together with thin strips of wet rawhide. Uncured leather shrinks when it dries, so the joints must have been satisfactorily tight. The leather was probably protected from moisture by coating it with varnish. Through the years, rod makers began to round off the square corners, and thus the ancestors of today's rods were born.

Several kinds of wood were favored for rod making until about the end of the 1700s, when bamboo appeared. The choice of rod makers in the pre-bamboo era was about equally divided between two tropical woods, greenheart and ironwood, but hickory and other woods were also used. These wooden rods were fearsome instruments, 16 to 20 feet long, and were weighed in pounds rather than ounces.

Casting in today's sense was not possible with early rods. Guides through which a line would flow freely did not enter the angling scene until the mid-1800s, so the fisherman was limited in distance to the length of his rod plus a line a few feet longer than the rod. Lack of suitable reels also made modern-style casting impractical. Reels—then called "windlasses"—were disks with a deep groove in their rims to store line and a center peg that slipped into a hole in the rod-butt. The reel's spool sat flat atop the butt of the rod instead of perching over it with the axle at right angles.

Even when the first bamboo rods began to replace those of hardwood in the late 1700s, casting had to wait for the rigid guide to be invented somewhere around 1850. The first guides were of the type called "ring and keeper," the keeper being a footed horseshoe-shaped wire wound to the rod, the ring through which the line ran flopping loose in the U-shaped keeper. Silk had come into use for lines by that time, replacing earlier lines made from braided horsehair, though horsehair leaders persisted for a number of years after silk lines began to be used. Nor did ironwood and greenheart rods disappear; some can still be seen on Irish and Scottish salmon streams, and in the making of saltwater rods, greenheart survived until well into the 20th century.

Real variety and control in rod design began with bamboo, and by the latter 1800s angling had entered its modern era of light, versatile tackle. Bamboo was the first genuinely controllable lightweight material rod makers had found. From it, rods with varied but predictable reflectance characteristics could be designed—reflectance being what we term action today. Balanced tackle and long casts still lay in the future, though. The first recorded world distance casting record, set in the 1880s in London, was a mere 43 feet.

Short rods came after fly rods had been in existence for a couple of decades. Until rigid guides became available, bamboo fly rods were used much like the older, heavy hardwood kind, to cast a line just a bit longer than the rod itself. The rigid guide made possible the short baitcasting rod, which was much more common than any other type in the early American angling scene. The multiplying reel, America's gift to angling, was in reasonably wide use by the mid-1850s, thus enabling casting barriers to be broken. As for material, bamboo reigned supreme in all kinds of rods for nearly a century and a half. During that time the craft of rod making was refined, and it was the master-workers of that long span of years who originated the prototypes of almost all of the kinds of rods in use today.

Like many crafts that are affected by continuing improvements in the materials they use, the making of fishing rods has always been a "state of the art" affair. This simply means that as each new material appears, it is followed by new designs and concepts. This has been true since the era of bamboo began, and it is equally true today. During some periods the changes are more drastic than during others, but there have been few times when rod making can be said to have been totally static.

World War II marked the end of bamboo's dominance as a rod material when fighting in China cut off the supply of Tonkin cane, which came from a relatively small area of that country. To replace Tonkin bamboo, makers turned to less familiar substances. These were usually metal alloys, with various copper-based mixtures the most common, and beryllium steel second. None of the metals proved very satisfactory. They were heavy, the rods made from them were sluggish and tended to fracture after short periods of use. When fiberglass appeared in the late 1940s it turned out to be the sought-for substitute.

So-called "glass" rods appeared in the very late 1940s, though several years were to pass before the evolution of the hollow fiberglass tubes in use today. Fiberglass is exactly what its name suggests, glass fibers or threads or filaments that are produced by forcing molten glass through dies perforated with tiny holes. It was from these filaments alone that the first glass rods were made, by embedding bundles of the fibers in a resin-based compound and molding them into cylinders. The cylinders were then ground to tapers on a centerless grinder.

As is true of many new, experimental products, the first glass rods were something less than perfect. They were heavy, badly balanced, clumsy to cast, soupy in action. Fishermen accustomed to the live, light springiness of bamboo were prone to go around muttering, "These damn things never will replace bamboo." Makers of the new rods were plagued not only by the problem of creating blades that had quickly responsive action, but by that of finding the correct embedding compound. After short use the original fiberglass rods often cracked, and tiny ends of the glass filaments worked themselves out of the embedding resin, giving the rod's surface a fuzzy look. These flaws were corrected when improved embedding and coating formulas were evolved, but initially they bedeviled the entire concept of glass rods for several years.

Today's tubular glass rods are produced by forming filaments covered with woven fiberglass fabric around a mandrel tapered to give the rod blank the desired wall thickness and action, applying a liquid resin coating, covering the coated mandrel with a form or mold that matches the mandrel's taper and curing the resin with controlled heat, under pressure. The process can be controlled in an almost infinite number of ways. The thickness of the walls of the blank can be varied at preselected points along its length; the fabric wrapping can be applied in different patterns; the characteristics of the resin bonding material can be varied; so can the gauge of the fiberglass filaments and the woven wrapping material.

Each manufacturer has a slightly different approach to the problem of creating the desired action. Some place the glass filaments in straight longitudinal lines and wrap them with a single strip of fabric that is also applied longitudinally; some apply the fiberglass wrapping in a spiral. In the Shakespeare Howald process, the inner filaments are applied in a diminishing spiral, and this is but one of the several patterns by which the raw materials are formed on the mandrels.

Whatever pattern is used in applying the glass materials to the mandrels, the manufacturing process is essentially the same. Dyes added to the adhesive give the blanks their color. The bonding under heat and pressure, and a period of curing, ultimately produce light, flexible, tapered tubes—rod blanks—that are predictably uniform in their actions.

Graphite rods are made from synthetic fibers of the same type of acrylic filaments as that used in weaving cloth for wearing apparel. The acrylic fibers are first baked at low temperatures, in the range of 570° F (300° C), then treated at higher temperatures, 2190°–2730° F (1200°–1500° C), in

which range the acrylic fibers are converted to carbon. After being carbonized, the material undergoes a second heat treatment at even higher
temperatures in ovens from which oxygen can be exhausted at a controlled
rate.

In this oxygen-free oven, the molecular structure of the carbonized
acrylic undergoes a transformation when the temperature range reaches
3630°–5430° F (2000–3000 C), and becomes crystalline graphite. At this
point the graphite fibers are long, loose filaments, elastic but delicate. They
are spread on an adhesive backing material for ease in handling, as technology has not yet discovered a way by which they can be woven into a fabric, as is fiberglass.

The graphite filaments are then transferred to the mandrel, coated with
resin, often encased in a fiberglass outer shell, and cured by essentially the
methods already described in relation to fiberglass rod-blank manufacture.
The resulting rod blank is extremely light, and highly resistant to breakage
resulting from repeated flexings. Fenwick, which pioneered graphite as a
rod material, has conducted flexing tests with bamboo, fiberglass, and
graphite rods. Bamboo fractured after slightly less than 30,000 flexes,
fiberglass failed at just over 290,000, while graphite blanks withstood
1,290,000 flexes, at which point the testing was stopped.

Fenwick's graphite rods appeared in the early 1970s and were advertised
as "H.M.G." graphite, the letters standing for High Modulus Graphite.
Even though copyrighted, the "H.M.G." designation was well on its way to
becoming a generic term applied to all graphite rods until the discovery
that graphite need not have a high modulus to be suitable for use in rod
blanks.

Let's dispose of that puzzling word, "modulus," before going any further. All substances have a maximum degree of bending or flexing before
they break, and "modulus" is the term applied to the degree of bending
characteristic to any given material. A 1-inch diameter cast-iron bar, for example, will break under weight before it bends; a forged steel bar will
deflect in fractions of an inch under the same amount of weight; a copper
bar will deflect still more. Thus, speaking relatively, cast iron has an extremely high modulus, steel a lower modulus, copper an even lower modulus. The word does not denote a specific degree of flexibility except when
applied to a specific material.

In fishing terms, graphite has approximately three times the modulus of
fiberglass. Suppose we take two rod blanks, one of high-modulus graphite,
the other of fiberglass. The blanks are identical in length, diameter, taper,
and wall thickness; identical in all respects except weight. The graphite
blank will be lighter than the one of fiberglass.

Now, we will find the performance characteristics of these two imaginary
blanks to be quite different. The graphite rod will be three times as stiff as
the fiberglass rod; that is, three times as much energy must be used to bend
the graphite blank into a curve identical with that of the fiberglass blank.
Low-modulus graphite in this same comparison test would require an identical expenditure of energy to bend it into an arc identical with that formed
by its fiberglass twin.

Still translating "modulus" into fishing terms, low-modulus materials will seldom be strained to the breaking point when a rod is in use. A fiberglass rod will seldom be worked to more than 35 or 40 percent of its maximum stress point; it reaches 50 percent of stress only when bent into a semicircle. Graphite rods, on the other hand, will reach approximately 70 percent of maximum stress when arced into a quarter-circle, though this figure will vary with the modulus of the graphite. Most graphite rods do reach maximum stress at a less extreme arc than does the lower-modulus fiberglass.

Makers compensate for these differences in several ways, varying wall thicknesses being the most common. Because of the extreme lightness of graphite, this does not result in an excessively heavy rod, or one that's unpleasantly stiff. Certainly none of the foregoing data should be taken as an implication that high-modulus graphite is unsuitable for use in rods. It has advantages. For example, a 2-ounce high-modulus graphite fly rod will handle a line of the same weight as a 4-ounce fiberglass or low-modulus graphite rod. And anglers are in general agreement that graphite rods have a more sensitive "feel" in recognizing strikes. In almost all respects, the characteristics of graphite closely match those of bamboo in rod-making applications.

Certainly graphite rods are long past the experimental stage; technology has advanced rapidly since their introduction in 1972. However, graphite has not had the impact on rod making that tubular fiberglass had in the 1950s, when it quickly replaced solid fiberglass. Rather, the introduction of graphite has spurred rod makers to develop vastly improved blanks of fiberglass and blends of graphite and fiberglass. The newest blanks come close to graphite in sensitivity, weight, and strength, and are priced only a little higher than what must now be called "regular" or "conventional" thick-walled fiberglass blanks.

Lamiglas has introduced a new thin-wall blank called S-Glass. Produced by a new process, the details of which haven't been publicly unfolded, Lamiglas S blanks are approximately 20 percent lighter, have a 25 percent higher modulus, and a 5 percent greater strength-to-weight ratio than their thick-walled blanks and are much more sensitive. The new blanks are available in baitcast, spincast, spinning, and fly models, in a wide selection of lengths. Their ferruling is the same as that used in Lamiglas graphite blanks. Their price is, of course, much lower than graphite.

Fenwick's new material, Fenglas, is a high-modulus fiberglass, some 34 percent above the modulus of their regular fiberglass blanks, but with only a bit less tensile strength than graphite. These blanks are ferruled with the tapered male-under-female ferrule used in Fenwick's graphite blanks. The Fenglas blanks are extremely sensitive and a fraction lighter than graphite. Fenglas blanks are available in all styles at prices that compare favorably with their conventional fiberglass blanks.

Shakespeare has gone the combination route in producing their Ugly Stik blanks, but still retain the Howald process in their construction. The Ugly Stik rods are made with the well-known spiral, this time of graphite fibers, with graphite fibers also used in combination with fiberglass as an outer layer. The graphite extends into the solid glass tip, which is bonded to the tubular bottom portion with a flexible epoxy. The result is a blank of excellent sensitivity and strength that has a truly remarkable flexibility.

No special tools or equipment are needed to work with any of the blanks made from these new materials. However, when you reach the stage of setting guides on a rod you're making, keep in mind that spacing is very important; don't try to duplicate spacings of guides on a favorite rod made of regular fiberglass. Remember, too, that small-diameter tips call for very light tiptops. Gary Loomis, Lamiglas production manager, recommends using the lightest tips possible not only on graphite, but on S-Glass rods. In testing a new fly rod, Gary found that a conventional stainless-steel pear-shaped tiptop was superior to the lightest ceramic insert tiptop in bringing out the rod's best action. As always when setting guides and tips, testing and experimenting pays off.

When making rods, it's impossible to consider the blanks used in isolation from other tackle, specifically reels and lines. A lot of anglers want to add new rods to their gear, but grow pale at the thought of matching a half-dozen new rods with an equal number of new reels. Dollar signs flash in front of their eyes like a computer going amok. Their anxiety is unwarranted, however, since most modern reels are versatile enough to be used with a group of rods.

One good freshwater baitcasting reel can be switched to almost any bait-cast rod, regardless of the rod's action, weight, or the test line or lure being used. Spincast and spinning reels aren't quite that flexible, but two carefully selected reels will serve three or four rods apiece. Except for the extremes in fly reels, the skeleton reels used on fairy fly rods and the heavy multiplying reels for salmon and saltwater fly rods, a couple of fly reels will serve a half-dozen rods each. In the medium range of rods, a single fly reel with a spool cavity into which weights can be placed will take care of all your needs. The point is that you don't need a separate reel for every rod in your collection.

In the chapters that are devoted later to specific types of rods, this subject will be explored in a little more detail. Here, it's enough just to note that you're going to want and need more than one kind of rod unless your fishing is of a very limited and specialized nature. Assembling a collection of rods by buying them across the counter can be a fairly expensive proposition, and making your own is the obvious answer to owning the variety you want without having to slap a mortgage on the old homestead.

You must select your own route to do-it-yourself savings. If you're planning to build only one rod, a kit will probably be your best bet, but if you've got your sights set on several rods of different kinds, you will pay even less than the cost of a good kit by ordering components in bulk. A kit will usually save you 20 to 25 percent of the cost of a ready-made bamboo rod, 40 to 45 percent on a graphite rod, and as much as 50 to 60 percent on a fiberglass rod. If you plan to make several rods, then check catalogs for bulk offers. A number of suppliers give discounts when you order as few as two or three blanks. Buying guides by the half-dozen or dozen is usually substantially more economical than buying only one or two, or a carded set. The same applies to reel seats, grip materials, and threads. Check suppliers' catalogs to see how bulk buying will save you money. In an appendix you'll find a list of firms selling rod-making components.

There are other advantages to making your own. In spite of the precision with which rod blanks are manufactured, each blank is an individual piece of workmanship. While all good-quality blanks—and most blanks today are of excellent quality—fit the basic specifications of action and weight under which they are sold, no two are precisely the same. The differences are tiny, usually indistinguishable, but they do exist. These differences are important when it comes to fitting the rod. A small difference in guide spacing, in setting the reel seat, can make a subtle difference in a blank's performance after it's become a rod. Factory work requires uniformity, working to prefigured averages, so all factory rods are fitted in exactly the same manner, the guides spaced identically, the reel seat in the same place, the grips and wrappings uniform.

You, on the other hand, can take time to experiment with each blank you use. You can test them with different guide spacings, different kinds of guides, different reel seat placements, until you get the action that suits you best. You can shorten a rod or make it longer; this will change its action, often significantly. Ferrule placement and grip contour also will change the action and performance of a rod. Only you can tune a rod to fit your hand and style of casting.

From the standpoint of fittings and wrappings, you can go one of two ways to get a rod that looks exactly as you want it to. You can have one made to your specifications by a custom rod maker, or you can make your own. The difference in cost between these two alternatives is even greater than between buying a factory rod and making your own. If you build it yourself, your rod will be unique, and you'll know exactly what's gone into its construction.

Finally, from the standpoint of use, there's an extra satisfaction in landing a fish with a rod you've made yourself. It's an extension of the feeling you get when you take a fish on a fly or lure that's your own handiwork. Don't ask me why this should be. It's one of the intangible, inexplicable things that fishermen feel. The sensation is akin to feeling the first lunge of an unseen fish taking fly or lure. You feel its power and you guess at its size, and you enjoy every minute of feeling that fish from strike to landing. This feeling is amplified when you've made the rod yourself, and it's a bonus that's repeated every time you use the rod.

So much for the preliminaries. Let's get on with the business—or pleasure—of rod making.

2

Getting Started

TOOLS

Equipping yourself to make fishing rods isn't as hard or as expensive as you might think. The same tools are used interchangeably on all types of rod blanks. Like stretch socks, "one size fits all." There are only a half-dozen essential tools, none of them expensive. If you want to do some jobs the very easiest way, you can put to good use a few others, and if you want to put together two or three time-saving, work-shortening jigs, you'll need a few tools usually found around most home workshops. The jigs can be made from scrap lumber and are optional. So are the tools not on the "essential" list.

Here are the essentials: a very fine-tooth saw such as the razor saws made by X-acto or their equivalent; a good cuticle nipper; a smooth-cut file, a rattail file, and a half-round mill bastard rough-cut file, and a knife file or triangular file.

Each of these has a specific function that it does better than any other tool. When cutting blanks of either fiberglass or graphite, you need the finest saw blade you can find, which is what razor saws offer. They have blades with 60 to 70 teeth per inch, while the finest hacksaw blades have about 20 to 25 teeth per inch, and will on occasion split or shred a blank. A coping saw with a 50- or 60-tooth-per-inch blade will do a good job, but coping saws are notoriously hard to handle in straight cuts. Jeweler's saws can be fitted with blades with up to 60 teeth per inch, but the razor saw is by far the easiest of all the alternatives to handle. It is also used in making skeleton reel seats and trimming cork grips.

A triangular file or knife file may be easier for you to use in cutting blanks than would a saw. The technique, illustrated in a later section, is to score the blank with the edge of the triangular file or the sharp edge of the knife file, and keep rotating the blank, deepening the scored line, until it separates. It's your option, use saw or file, whichever is handiest for you.

A lot of very good rod makers use skill knives or fly-tying scissors or even razor blades to trim loose ends of winding thread. Scissors always seem to leave an excess tag of thread that has to be singed off, while with knife or razor blade there's the danger of a slip that will cut the finished winding. The virtue of cuticle nippers is that they will trim flush with the winding but won't cut into it, and leave no tags of frizzies to bother you. It takes only one perfect winding spoiled by a knife-tip or one finger sliced with a razor blade to convince you of the advantage of a cuticle nipper.

Files might be called the indispensable of indispensables in rod making. You'll use a smooth file to taper guide feet, to remove excess glue, to smooth the ragged edges of sawn blanks, to work grips and reel seats. The half-round mill bastard roughs-in cork grips quickly and doesn't tear cork as a coarse rasp will, while its rounded side makes contouring a grip very easy. The rattail file is a must for reaming reel seat bushing and grips and winding checks.

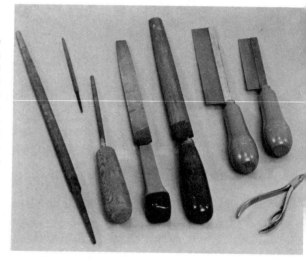

Basic tools for rod making are few and simple. From left: Files are the most important tools you'll use, and you need large and small or medium-sized rat-tails, a triangular file, a smooth-cut and a half-round mill bas-tard for rough work. You will find razor saws very handy—hacksaw blades are too coarse to work on fiberglass or graph-ite. Cuticle nippers work much better than manicure or fly-tying scissors in trimming threads.

If you own an electric drill you'll find it useful in forming and finishing grips, but you can get along without it. Some kind of drill is needed if you're going to fit a butt or hosel on a rod, but even this can be done with a hand drill.

Another optional accessory that's very nice to have if you're going to make more than one or two rods is a winding rest. You can wind rods quite easily freehand. I've done many of them this way, with a fly-tying bobbin holding the thread. I've also used the technique of maintaining tension on winding thread by pulling it through the pages of a book. However, a winding rest gives you an extra hand, and it's easy to make one from scrap lumber. Just recently, I built the most efficient rest I've ever used. It has as its key feature rollers from an office photocopy machine attached to thin pieces of plywood on each side; it's one of the three types of winding rests shown in the pictures. The paper advance rollers, as they are known, you can get at any office supply or stationery store that services photocopy machines for a nickle or dime each, or used ones may be given to you free.

The rollers in these machines must be replaced at intervals, and the used ones work for winding rests just as satisfactorily as new ones. Attached to the plywood supports by a bolt and a pair of washers, these rollers support a rod section firmly without marring its surface or allowing it to slip or slide. Furniture casters, often used in this kind of winding rest, generally roll too freely to be really satisfactory.

Winding rests are handy, but not essential. The two shown here can be made quickly from scrap lumber and odds and ends. The one in the foreground has pieces of heavy clothesline wire bent and pushed into slightly undersized holes in the base; the U-ends that hold the rod are covered with short lengths of surgical tubing, to prevent scratching, but masking tape would serve as well. The one in the rear has strips of self-stick weather stripping in its uprights' vees. Normal working height for most people is 11 to 13 inches above the table or bench top, but you can tailor the height to whatever suits your own arms the best.

Total cost of this roller-equipped rest was less than 50¢ for wing-nuts and cup hooks. All thread spools slip onto ¼-inch dowel stock. Surgical tubing sections between the spools act as retainers and friction brakes to control thread tension. An outrigger, not shown, bent from heavy wire, supports long sections of a rod when you must work on the tip or butt end.

SUPPLIES

Your supply list for rod building is even shorter than the list of tools, and the items on it aren't costly. You'll need sandpaper in three grades, #36, #80, and #120. The most satisfactory I've found is open-faced garnet cabinet paper, which is resistant to filling or clogging when used on cork. You'll also need #400 wet-or-dry auto body paper, a sheet of crocus cloth, and a roll of masking tape. All these are available at lumber yards, hardware stores, and machine supply houses. You'll be more likely to find crocus cloth at one of the latter. It's technically classed as an abrasive but is really more of a polishing material. Crocus cloth is used much like sandpaper but removes material in almost microscopic quantities. Sandpaper or emery paper even in the finest grades are too coarse to be used on such metal rod fittings as ferrules and guides. Only crocus cloth will smooth away surface irregularities without harming or scratching a plated surface, or affecting the close metal-to-metal fit of ferrules.

Add to your supplies three kinds of adhesives: a waterproof glue of the resorcinol-based type, a waterproof cement that can be softened by heat, and epoxy. Each of these has its place in rod making. Waterproof resorcinol-based glue is the best adhesive for gluing up cork rings into grips. All the others I've tried, most of them with a neoprene or methyl-ethyl-ketone base, fuzz up along the glue line when used to join cork rings. Borden and Carter both make very good waterproof glues that leave almost invisible glue lines on the completed grips. Both must be mixed just before use and have a working life of about two hours, depending on temperature and humidity. Both require overnight or 24 hours to set up firmly.

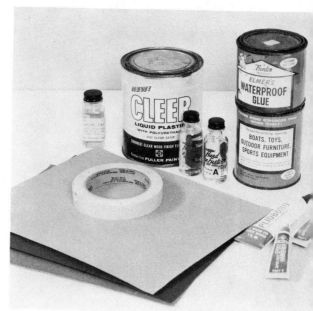

Expendable supplies for rod building include sandpaper in at least three grades, from #80 to #400 wet-or-dry auto body paper; adhesives; waterproof glue; masking tape; color preservative; and a finishing varnish such as Cleer or epoxy.

For setting reel seats and ferrules and grips, the neoprene- and ketone-based adhesives do an excellent job. Both types give good adhesion on slick graphite blanks. Goodyear's Pliobond, 3M's Super-Strength, Borden's Heavy-Grip cement, Featherweight's Custom-Bond Glue are about equally satisfactory. Reel seats and ferrules are set by many rod makers with epoxy, but I shy away from this practice. Reel seats and ferrules are the rod fittings most susceptible to damage, the ones that must be replaced now and then. All the adhesives mentioned above soften when heated, allowing a damaged ferrule or tiptop or reel seat to be removed easily; fittings set with epoxy must be filed off.

Epoxy has its uses, to be sure. It is invaluable for setting butt ferrules on baitcast/spincast rods, and on heavy saltwater rods. It's also a good adhesive for installing glass-to-glass ferrules, and for fitting butt and joint plugs. However, when installing a plug of this kind on a graphite blank, especially a long plug with a close fit, I generally prefer an adhesive that retains its flexibility when set.

Stick ferrule cement is another material that can be softened by heat, and for many years was the only adhesive used for ferrules and tiptops and, generally, for reel seats as well. This material has one major disadvantage, though. You must set the fitting very quickly, while the cement is still hot, which means handling the tiptop or ferrule or reel seat with pliers or with a cloth to protect your hands from the heated metal. This makes for clumsy working conditions, and the cement sets up so fast that often a fitting's position can't be adjusted without reheating the work. Most of the adhesives with a neoprene or methyl-ethyl-ketone base give you as long as two minutes to align a reel seat or tiptop before the cement begins to set. For instant field repairs, of course, stick ferrule cement is very handy, as it's compact to carry, and a fitting installed with it can be used at once without waiting for the cement to set or to dry.

BLANKS

At the top of your materials list are the blanks you'll be using as the base for that new rod. Blanks are just what their name implies—unfitted rods. They're also called "blades," so if you encounter this term later on, don't let it throw you. Blanks are as many and various as individual fingerprints; they range from delicate to sturdy, small to large.

Many manufacturers' catalogs will list up to 150 different kinds of blanks. These will include blanks for baitcast/spincast, spinning, fly, surf, boat/pier, trolling, and other types of rods. While the manner of listings will vary in different catalogs, you'll usually find such information as the type of rod for which the blank is designed; its length, tip diameter in 64ths of an inch, butt diameter in decimal fractions; weight; whether it is one-piece or factory-ferruled. Listings for one-piece blanks often include the midpoint diameter in 64ths of an inch, to guide you in ordering a ferrule. No blanks are pictured because you can't tell much about them from a photo.

Some catalogs list the components you'll need to make up your rod, but usually this information is contained only in catalogs from suppliers who sell complete kits. A few blank manufacturers will sell at retail from their factories, but most will not. This information will be found in an appendix listing manufacturers and suppliers.

Featherweight, Fenwick, Lamiglas, Orvis, and Shakespeare make both graphite and fiberglass blanks. Orvis also has split bamboo blanks. Scientific Anglers makes only graphite fly rod blanks, Sabre and St. Croix only fiberglass. Childre-Fuji features fiberglass but is getting into graphite. You'll find blanks from any of these makers quite satisfactory.

Remember that a number of manufacturers sell only through retail dealers and in some cases their products will bear a dealer's house brand name instead of the maker's. Consult catalogs from both manufacturers and dealers to learn what's available. The appendix just mentioned lists firms supplying catalogs.

In later chapters devoted to individual types of rods, you'll find suggestions that should help you in choosing the blank that will make up to the kind of rod you have in mind.

FERRULES

Many blank manufacturers give you a choice between one-piece and factory-ferruled blanks. The typical factory-ferruled fiberglass blank has a plug of solid fiberglass fitted into one end of the mating sections and ground to fit perfectly into a sleeve on the other. The joint may be straight-walled or taper-walled. This is also true of graphite blanks, with the single exception of those made by Scientific Anglers, which have an internal female ferrule of aluminum bonded into the lower section and the mating male ferrule bonded into the upper half of the blank.

Which section of the blank becomes the male and which the female is pretty much a matter of maker's choice. Shakespeare and Lamiglas sleeve the bottom sections of their blanks to make a female ferrule, and the male ferrule is formed on the upper section. Fenwick puts the sleeve on the upper section of the blank. Featherweight—or Rawhide, the brand name of this firm's blanks—fits no self-ferrules, but uses the company's own Sizmatic aluminum ferrules. Fiberglass rods made by Lamiglas and Sabre have an internal flexible ferrule of fiberglass rather than the taper-and-sleeve fitting. The St. Croix Corporation uses conventional metal ferrules on its fiberglass blanks.

Fitting a one-piece blank with a ferrule is not a hard task, though it appears so to a lot of novice rod makers. Ferruling a blank adds a small amount of time to the job, but requires no more skill or care than any other of the operations you'll encounter. You can also install your own glass-to-glass ferrules in little more time than is required to fit a pair of metal ferrules. This will be covered in a later chapter.

If you decide on metal ferrules you have a lot of choices. The least costly are brass plated with nickel or chrome, the most popular are anodized aluminum. The longest wearing ferrules are nickel-silver, but these are very hard to find and weigh more than either of those mentioned above. Even heavier, by today's graphite and fiberglass blank comparisons, are ferrules of alloy bronze and German silver, though a few trickle into the United States from Europe to supply some of the dwindling number of custom rod makers.

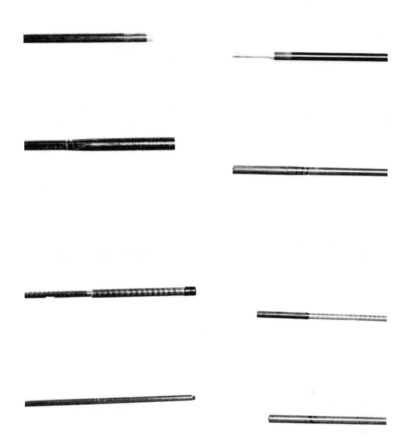

Factory ferrules, from top: Scientific Anglers' all-metal internal ferrule, which has a tiny screw at the bottom of the female socket; Lamiglas graphite, which has a sleeved female section on the butt of the blank; Shakespeare graphite, which has a sleeved but not tapered female ferrule on the butt; Fenwick, which has a sleeved female ferrule on the upper half of the blank and a Morse-tapered male section on the butt.

Consider the service that will be expected from the rod you're making before choosing its ferrules. If it's an ultralight fly or spinning rod, then you'll want the lightest and most delicate ferrules you can get, in other words aluminum. Plated brass or nickel silver are fine for heavier rods, and I'm still old-fashioned enough to want chromed or nickeled ferrules on any rod that will be used for saltwater fishing. Milt Stevens, the head man at Featherweight Products, producers of Sizmatic ferrules, points out with justification that my feeling in this matter is prejudice, and I'll admit it is.

However, a lot of the early aluminum ferrules and reel seats were used and found wanting on saltwater rods before the anodizing process as we know it today came into being. Milt points to the seaplanes that are made of modern anodized aluminum to prove his contention, and sometimes even comes close to shaking my prejudice, but habits are hard to overcome. Even the Featherweight Sizmatic had its problems during the early stages of its development, though now it is as satisfactory a ferrule as you'll find. One of the nice things about aluminum ferrules is that they can be had in colors to match almost any blank or winding thread. Of course, this really isn't any problem when you fit a rod with plated ferrules, since you can just carry the winding thread up to the welt on the female and down to the shoulder on

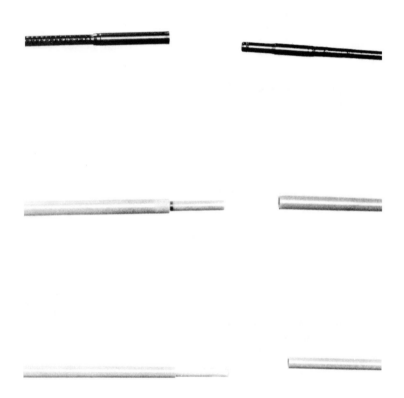

More ferrules, from top: Rawhide's own metal Sizematic O-ring ferrule, on both graphite and fiberglass blanks; Sabre, which has a flexible male ferrule on the butt section and a reinforced female section on the top half of the fiberglass blank; and Lamiglas's fiberglass blank ferrule, which also uses a cylindrical male ferrule on the bottom section of the blank.

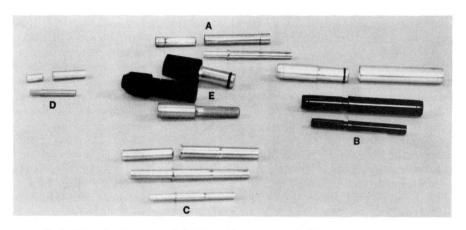

Typical ferrules that you might fit on blanks yourself: **(A)** unwelted, straight English-style chromed brass; **(B)** welted, shouldered nickeled brass; **(C)** three Sizmatic O-ring ferrules, the top one unjointed to show its construction; **(D)** Allan chromed brass, shouldered mini-ferrules for light rods; **(E)** Featherweight's Sizmatic push-ferrule for baitcast blanks; Childre-Fuji's similar O-ring push-ferrule fitting its handles; and Featherweight's knurled butt ferrule to fit chuck-and-collet grips.

the male if you want to avoid the shine of plating. Wrapping a ferrule won't affect the action of a rod.

Mini-ferrules, or micro-ferrules, as they're sometimes called, are shorter and lighter than conventional ferrules. The claim made for these abbreviated ferrules is that they weigh less and also shorten the flat spot that any kind of ferrule is going to create in a rod. After replacing standard ferrules on a couple of light rods with micro-ferrules, I wasn't able to discern any difference in the action. However, I've never tried them on ultralight rods, as it's my conviction that these short, very delicate rods should either be one-piece or self-ferruled. Mini-ferrules might well make a significant difference on extremely light blanks.

Ferrules are sized in 64ths of an inch, pending our national conversion to the metric system, the size quoted being the inside diameter (ID) of the female ferrule. The tube of the male ferrule is now almost universally shouldered above the point where it stops when fully inserted into the female, and the shouldered portion is normally $1/64$ inch smaller in diameter than the tube of the female. Thus, if you have a rod requiring an $18/64$-inch ferrule, this is the inside diameter of the tube of the female—the tube being the portion that fits to the rod—and the outside diameter (OD) of the plug portion of the male will also be $18/64$ inch. The portion of the male ferrule into which the blank is inserted will be $17/64$ inch, just right for a snug fit after the bottom $1/4$ to $3/8$ inch of the blank has been reduced slightly by sanding.

Different styles of factory self-ferruling have already been discussed, so now let's look briefly at the kind of glass-to-glass ferrule you can install yourself. Basically, it consists of a short length of solid fiberglass rod inserted in the bottom section of a blank and carefully reduced to a taper that matches that of the inner wall of the upper section of the blank. The blank on both sides of the joint is reinforced by wrapping, sometimes by putting on a thin metal ring to keep the joint from belling. This type of ferrule is not suitable for use on graphite blanks, and I wouldn't recommend its use on heavy-duty fiberglass rods. Full details of its fitting are in a later chapter. It's not an especially difficult job but is one that requires you to work carefully.

There is one more type of ferrule that you will use in making rods, and that is the butt ferrule used on short baitcast/spincast rods fitted with detachable grips. This ferrule's upper portion is sized in 64ths of an inch ID to fit the blank's butt, while its lower portion may be a serrated plug to fit a chuck, or a straight plug with an O-ring to be pushed for a friction-fit into the handle.

GRIPS AND HANDLES

Freshwater rods have grips, saltwater rods have handles, if you're wondering about the difference in nomenclature.

Traditionally, grips on freshwater spinning and fly rods are made from cork rings glued together and sanded to the desired contour; baitcast/spincast rods are generally fitted with a preformed grip and integral reel seat into which the blade is inserted. These are variously straight or offset handled or have pistol-grips or hand-contoured grips.

There's no really tricky work involved in gluing and forming a grip from cork rings. If you want to save a bit of tedious waiting for glued-up rings to dry, you can buy cork "sticks"—ready-glued rings in several choices of ID and OD—or you can buy preformed cork grips in several styles. The disadvantage of using totally preformed grips is that you're limited to about four styles, while if rings or sticks are used, your choice of contours is limitless. Methods of using rings, sticks, and preformed grips are given later.

Since the advent of preshaped foam plastic grips, many spinning and baitcast/spincast rods are being fitted with these slip-on grips, and they're also beginning to be used on fly rods. Foam grips were popular at the outset for use on heavy saltwater rods. A majority of surf rods, most boat rods, and virtually all heavy trolling rods have either a full set of foam grips, or at least a preformed foam foregrip. To my knowledge, Featherweight Products is the sole producer of these, under their trade names of Foamlite and Hypalon.

Traditionally the grips of boat/pier and trolling rods have been made of ash, but these are now being replaced by foam grips over a steel core in the case of boat/pier rods and either aluminum or stainless steel in the cast of boat rods. On both these types of saltwater rods, however, a plastic foregrip is usual.

When selecting a grip or handle for a blank, there are a number of factors to be considered. The foremost is comfort, the weight being next. Often, the difference between a rod that's easy and comfortable to cast, a rod having the intangible quality that can only be described as "a good

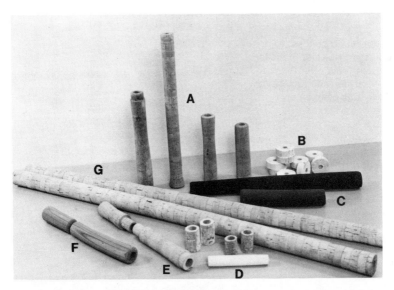

Some of the grips available to the rod maker: **(A)** preformed cork grips for spinning and fly rods, sold by most dealers in rod-making supplies; **(B)** cork rings for forming your own grips; **(C)** Featherweight's Foamlite and Hypalon slip-on grips; **(D)** reel seat bushings of cork and wood; **(E)** completely preformed cork grip with integral bushings; **(F)** Gladdings' slip-on foam plastic Glad grips; **(G)** cork sticks, which save the trouble of gluing rings together.

feel," and one that's clumsy or awkward to handle can be traced to the grip.

If your hands are exceptionally large or small, you may find the standard grips on factory-made rods difficult to hold easily. The cure, of course, is to experiment with different contours until you've hit on one that's perfect for you. Each rod seems to have individual characteristics, and these often require grips of special shapes. Even slight variations in diameter and contour will make a great deal of difference in the ease with which you handle a given rod. Often as little as a $1/16$-inch change in the grip diameter or an equally small change in its contour will convert a problem rod to a pleasant one to use.

On very light fly and spinning rods, cork is the most versatile material to use. On such rods, the reel seat is often no more than a grooved section of the grip in which the reel feet fit and sliding rings are provided to hold the reel in place. A cellulite slip-on grip introduced by Gladding appears to have possibilities as a preformed grip for rods of these types, however, as it can be formed to different contours. Preformed foam grips work well on heavy spinning and saltwater rods, of course. As for the handles on heavy saltwater boat/pier and trolling rods, unless you have access to a supply of well-seasoned ash and a woodworking ship equipped with a lathe, you're better advised to buy factory-made handles.

There are a few miscellaneous fittings associated with grips and handles. Butt caps of rubber, plastic, or metal are used to finish off the ends of all

Top left, Childre baitcast grips; bottom right, Rawhide baitcast grips. Both firms offer these in different styles and colors to match various blanks.

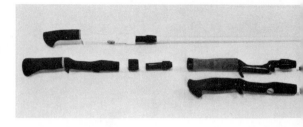

Traditional ash handles for saltwater rods. The Varmac handle, top, has a rubber butt cap. The Allan handle, below, is fitted with a gimbal for a fighting harness.

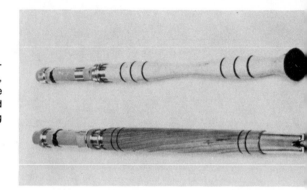

Miscellaneous fittings available from most tackle shops: **(A)** Screw-in and slip-on butt caps; **(B)** traditional hook keeper and Allan's combination hook keeper/leader cutter; **(C)** metal and plastic winding checks; **(D)** hosels, or fancy butt-pieces.

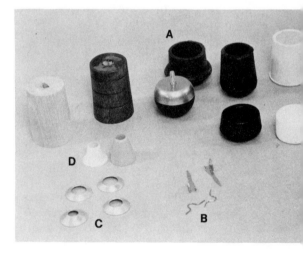

rod handles; on light rods, the butt cap may be made of cork. Hosels, also used to finish rod butts, are glorified butt caps; these have become ornamental as well as functional, adding a decorative touch to a rod. Some rods have hosels at the top of the grip, replacing the traditional grip check or winding check, which is usually a metal or plastic ring or small sleeve. Fancy hosels can be made from layers of hardwood or plastic disks at small cost and in very little time.

REEL SEATS

There are five kinds of reel seats, though many materials are used in making them. Open-end reel seats are used on rods with both foregrip and butt grip, and are mounted between the two. Fly rod reel seats have one closed end, and are mounted at the bottom of the rod butt. On heavy rods, an extension that plugs into the bottom of the reel seat may be provided; when it is not in use a button slips into the end of the seat. Baitcast/spincast rods are usually fitted with handles having integral reel seats. Light fly and spinning rods may have cork reel seats, with metal bands at top and bottom providing the threads for the hood that holds the reel foot. Such rods may also be fitted with shroud or skeleton reel seats that can be moved along the grip.

Plastic reel seats with plastic locking rings; plastic barrel reel seats with metal locking rings or hoods; aluminum, nickel-plated brass, and chrome-plated brass are all available. Your choice should be made not only by your own preference, but by the type of rod to which the reel seat is being fitted. Except in the case of ultralight rods, where a set of retaining rings or a shroud reel seat is usually preferable, weight is seldom a factor to be considered. Most freshwater reel seats weigh within a fraction of an ounce of one another, whether they're of anodized aluminum or plastic. Tough, modern plastics relieve you of worry over wear and breakage, so use them wherever they seem indicated.

Light saltwater rods and specialty rods such as muskie rods and heavy steelhead spinning rods are generally fitted with sturdy nickel- or chrome-

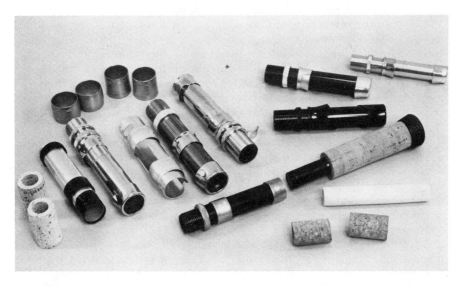

Spinning-reel seats and bushings are at left, fly-rod reel seats and bushings at right. A shroud or skeleton seat for light spinning rods is in the center of that group of reel seats; the rings above are retainers for all-cork grips with integral reel grooves. In the fly-rod reel-seat array, at bottom, is a reel seat with an extension or "fighting" grip; when in normal use a button plugs the reel seat's open end.

plated reel seats. Handles fitted to heavy boat/pier rods and regulation tackle trolling rods have a reel seat built into them, which settles that problem automatically. Generally speaking, use these plated reel seats on any rod that's going to be exposed to saltwater or tidal waters.

Except for the last type named, reel seats are fitted to the rod over cork or wooden bushings that compensate for the difference between the inside diameter of the seat and the outside diameter of the blank. Standard inside diameters for freshwater reel seats are $5/8$ and $3/4$ inch, though you can find $1/2$-inch ID seats for light rods. The ID of saltwater seats is $5/8$ and $7/8$ inch.

All the details needed to fit reel seats are given in Chapter 3 or in the chapters devoted to individual types of rods.

GUIDES AND TIPTOPS

Today, guides form a very large and varied family. There are specialized guides for every type of rod, and while guides are often interchangeable, you should take great care in your selections. The guides you fit on a blank will play a tremendously important part in the functioning of the finished rod. In order to make an intelligent choice, you should be reasonably well acquainted with the variety that's available.

All guides can be divided into three basic kinds: ring, snake, and roller. Ring guides with aluminum oxide or ceramic ring inserts lead in popularity today for baitcast/spincast rods, as these insert materials are very slick and reduce line friction to a noticeable degree, while at the same time being very resistant to line-scoring. The second choice of ring guides for freshwater rods is the type having tungsten carbide rings; these are somewhat lighter than the insert type but are a bit less friction-free and are very hard to score. Tungsten carbide rings are also very widely used on spinning rods, where the greater weight of insert guides becomes a factor.

Boat/pier rods are also fitted with ring guides, usually of the center-braced type for extra strength. Hard chrome-plated guides are perhaps the most satisfactory for this kind of rod. The metal is very highly rust-resistant, though not quite as hard as ceramic or tungsten carbide; the latter metal is prone to rusting when used in salt or tidal waters.

Snake guides, which take their name from their sinuous humped shape, are the traditional fitting for fly rods, except for the butt or stripper guide, which is a ring guide. There is a growing tendency today to fit ceramic insert guides as the butt guide on fly rods, and on rods of $8^1/_2$ feet or greater length, it's now an accepted practice to fit a second ring guide above the stripper guide, before beginning the series of snake guides that are spaced to the tip of the rod.

Saltwater trolling rods are fitted with roller guides, high-precision mechanisms featuring a caged roller or series of rollers that revolve on a miniature axle on tiny ball bearings. Naturally, such guides are heavy in relation to those with which freshwater and lighter saltwater rods are equipped, but the trolling rods are heavy, too. Roller guides are essential when wire lines are to be used on a rod. Metal lines will score any metal except tungsten carbide in a very short time, and as already noted, this metal does not stand up well in salt water.

There are several specialty guides that need to be mentioned here for your consideration. For spinning rods—and recommended by their maker for fly rods as well—are one-piece stainless-steel ring guides manufactured by Gudebrod and marketed under the trademarked name of Aetna Foulproof Guides. In these guides, ring and feet are formed from a single length of metal, and the foot is formed on a slant that reduces line-fouling. These guides are light in weight and extremely flexible; they flex with the rod and reduce flat spots quite substantially, especially on light rods.

Childre-Fuji offers a slip-on guide that has no feet and requires no winding to bind it to the rod. These guides are made in the form of a figure eight, the bottom loop of the guide being slipped on the rod and set with a dab of adhesive. The top ring has a ceramic insert, and both rings are graduated in sizes so that they can be spaced properly along a rod. The same firm also offers a large-ring spinning rod guide that folds flat on the rod for carrying. Mildrum also makes a fold-down spinning rod guide series.

Lightweight ceramic insert guides with a single foot are another of Childre-Fuji's offerings. These guides are being fitted experimentally on heavy fly rods to reduce line friction and the line cling that is often encountered with fly rod snake guides. The maker recommends these single-foot guides for graphite rods, to give these rods increased flexibility, which results from a single winding being required to bind them in place.

Tiptops vary in type almost as greatly as guides. They range from simple loops of wire set into a solid barrel, used on fly rods, to the intricately engineered roller tops with which saltwater trolling rods are fitted. Spinning, spincast/baitcast, boat/pier, and heavy-duty fly rods are generally fitted with braced tiptops. For light fly rods, a simple loop tiptop of tungsten carbide is the best choice. Braced tiptops with tungsten carbide rings are generally used on light spinning rods. Ceramic insert guides are now favored for heavy fly rods, and braced tiptops with inserts for heavy spinning and baitcast/spincast rods. Stainless-steel or hard-chrome plate braced tiptops belong on boat/pier rods, and of course the heavy regulation tackle (RT) saltwater rods require roller tiptops.

For many years, ring guides have been sized in terms of their inside ring diameter expressed in 64ths of an inch. Now, the metric system is changing this. Allan Tackle Co. has started to size its guides in millimeters and to measure them in terms of the ring's outside diameter, a practice formerly followed only by Mildrum. Look for this to become increasingly common as use of the metric system spreads. There will be a transition period during which both 64ths of an inch and millimeters will be listed, then the 64ths measurement can be expected to fade away.

Tiptops are sized by the inside barrel diameter in 64ths of an inch, but this, too, can be expected to change as use of metric measurements becomes general. Inasmuch as the tip of your rod is both the most delicate area and gets the greatest strain, it should not be necessary to emphasize the importance of fitting a tiptop of exactly the right inside diameter on any rod you make. Sanding or scraping the tip of the blank should be avoided.

How many guides does a rod need? That question will be answered in a later chapter and in chapters dealing with various types of rods. Some short

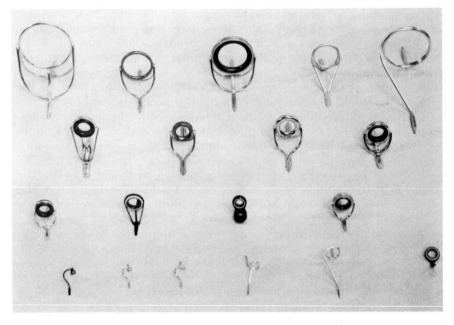

A sampling of freshwater guides.

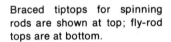
Braced tiptops for spinning rods are shown at top; fly-rod tops are at bottom.

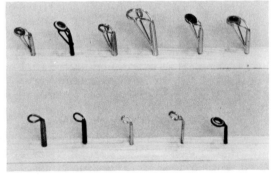

baitcast rods may require as few as four guides for best performance, a long fly or spinning rod may need nine or more. Heavy-wall blanks will usually require one guide more than thin-wall blanks of equal length to bring out the rod's best action. That's the only rule of thumb that I can offer here; fitting guides to a rod is a highly individual proposition.

It's impossible to emphasize too strongly the importance of choosing good-quality guides of the proper type for any rod in which you're going to invest your time and money. The difference in price between second-grade guides and those of the highest quality is very small indeed. Cheap guides can be identified at a glance. Their surface looks rough instead of mirror-smooth, the feet are coarsely tapered and have large bottom ridges that must be filed away to give a smooth foot-to-blank fit, and often there will be tiny flecks of plating metal on the rings. Close examination may reveal rough spots that will scrape and weaken your line.

In contrast, high-quality guides have finely tapered feet with small ridges on their bottoms. All surfaces are glass-smooth, joints are neatly finished, and the entire guide has a polished sparkle. Even the finest guides will require a little bit of handwork before they are fitted to a blank, but this work is minimized when top-grade guides are used.

THREADS

Last on our materials list, but far from being the least important, are the threads you will use in winding your rod. Most rod-winding thread today is made of hot-stretch nylon, which is resilient but not stretchy or elastic. If you want to use silk, the traditional winding thread, Gudebrod has fly-tying silk in several colors that is suitable for winding light rods. But please remember that rod-winding thread is not the same as sewing thread, and keep peace in the household by ignoring the temptation to raid your wife's sewing basket.

Nylon winding thread is available in a rainbow of hues, including two-tone threads offering one or more contrasting or complementing colors. Use heavy thread, designated EE or E, for big heavy-duty rods; thread sizes diminish through D, C, A, and down to O and OO, which is the finest practical diameter. Sizes D and C are right for most rods, the smaller diameters being reserved for delicate light and ultralight blanks. A 50-yard spool of size E will wrap ten to twelve rods.

Even in shades of black and white you can judge the array of colors available for winding rods. The big spools hold one ounce, which translates into roughly 1200 yards of size A, 575 yards of D, 400 yards of E, and 265 yards of EE. The small spools in the left foreground hold 50 yards regardless of thread diameter, and the tiny spool holds 15 yards, or about enough to wind the trim on an average rod. Gudebrod's Butt Wind, in right foreground, is a braided strip used in applying spiral and diamond butt decorative touches.

If you want to put on a fancy butt trim, Gudebrod has a butt wrap that is much easier to handle when forming wide spiral or diamond patterns than are single threads. It's available in a variety of single or mixed colors.

Several kinds of thin, colored plastic rod-winding tapes are on the market, but I cannot recommend their use except as an under-wrap where a strip of contrasting color is desired to show up a decorative spiral finish-wrap. These tapes do not have the strength or permanence required for winding on guides. Even under a protective varnish coating, those I've used have worked loose in a relatively short time, and have now been replaced with thread windings.

We'll go into winding techniques later on.

For quick reference, here is what you'll need in the way of materials:

Rod blank	Butt cap or hosel
Ferrules, unless factory-fitted	Winding check (grip check)
Grip or cork rings	Guides
Reel-seat bushings	Tiptop
Reel seat	Thread

With these materials and the tools and supplies listed earlier, even a fumble-fingered fisherman with two left thumbs set backward on his hands can make a rod that's not merely presentable, but unique and pleasant to use. There's an old saying taught me by a very skilled carpenter who shared with me the secrets of his craft more years ago than I like to remember. I'd sawed a board off too short, and the carpenter stood looking at me with an unhappy frown. "Remember this," he told me. "Measure twice, and you'll only have to cut once."

Measuring twice and being sure your fittings match the rod blank is more important in rod making than carpentry. But, if you make a mistake, it can always be cured. It'll just take a little more time.

3

Basic Procedures

ALMOST ALL THE basic procedures followed in rod making are common to all types of rods. These include setting ferrules, forming and fitting grips, setting reel seats, fitting tiptops, and winding guides. The operations, tools, materials, and other aspects of these jobs are essentially the same, whether you're working on a cane pole, a fairy fly rod, a saltwater spinning rod, or a regulation tackle trolling rod.

We'll cover in this chapter all of the basic procedures, and reserve differences for later chapters in which we'll go into full details of fitting the types of individual blanks that become baitcast/spincast, spinning, fly, and other types of rods. If you're starting your first rod-making venture, then be sure to consult not only this chapter, but the preceding chapter and the chapter devoted to the specific kind of rod you're making. While in most cases you'll be perfectly safe in using the procedures this chapter covers on any kind of blank, there might be some detail that you'd miss if you didn't check the appropriate chapter.

All the procedures covered here will be in the sequence that they should be performed when actually working on your blank. If you didn't choose a factory-ferruled blank, the first job is to set a ferrule or ferrules. Next comes the grip, then the reel seat—which in many cases will be a part of the grip—and at this point you must stop to test the blank for guide spacing. After the correct spacing for your blank has been determined, you'll wind on the guides, add whatever decorative touches you wish, such as a butt wind, and, finally, finish the job by varnishing or epoxy-coating the windings.

Before you do any actual building, or put anything at all on your blank, though, there's an important first step you must undertake. Like laying the foundation on which a building rests, if this first step is taken carefully, you'll have a true base on which to work as you convert your blank into a finished rod. Don't omit it.

FIRST STEP – LOCATING THE SPINE

When a tubular blank is manufactured it is formed on a tapered mandrel that has been covered with the fibers of glass or graphite that give the blank its flexible resilience, its action. These fibers are surrounded by a flexible resin that has been covered with a fiberglass mesh or cork. This is common to all tubular fiberglass blanks, but not to all graphite blanks. Some graphite blanks are made by wrapping the fiber-coated mandrel spirally with a heat-shrinking tape instead of a mesh or cloth.

On all blanks having a mesh or cloth coating over the inner fibers, a thin line of overlap is formed where the ends of the mesh come together. This line is generally invisible, especially on blanks with an opaque outer finish, but it is there. Its effect is most pronounced on thin-wall fiberglass blades, and on spirally wrapped graphite blanks the effect on action may be microscopically small.

This line of overlap makes a plane which forms the "spine" of the blank. A less pronounced second spine occurs on the opposite side of the blank, 180° from the true spine. Guides must be set along one of these two longitudinal planes, or the finished rod will probably have a twisty, soupy, unpredictable action. The reel must also be set along this line in order to be aligned with the guides.

Opinions vary as to the best side along which to set the guides. Some rod makers place them on the true spine, others 180° opposite it, on the false spine, feeling this to be the "strong" side of the blank. I don't know of any scientific basis for favoring one side over the other, and think the choice is primarily a matter of personal opinion. My own preference is to set the guides on the spine itself on baitcast/spincast and heavy-duty rods, but to set the guides opposite the spine on fly rods and spinning rods. My logic in forming this opinion might be flawed, but it seems to me that rods with the guides in these settings give better performance both in casting and in playing a fish, as well as having a greater delicacy of "feel."

Whatever your choice is, you must locate the blank's spine and mark it for future reference before sawing it to set ferrules or performing any other operations such as fitting reel seat, guides, and so on. There are three methods of locating the spine, and you might find it worthwhile to try them all, then decide which you prefer.

Method one calls for a table or bench. Lay the blank over an edge with about half to two-thirds of its butt hanging free. Holding the tip in your fingers, rotate the blank slowly. Let it roll along the edge of the support; this is easier than to try to hold it in a fixed spot. At some point in its rotation, the blank will seem to resist turning, then will suddenly jump to complete a rotation. You might have to go through several revolutions before you notice this, unless the rod is butt-heavy. However, after several rotations of the blank, you'll begin looking for this "springy" spot, and where it occurs, the spine will be at the bottom of the blank. If you're working with a very light blank, you might have to weight the butt with a few wraps of wire solder to be sure you're feeling the hesitation followed by the springy "jump."

The second method is to rest the butt of the blank on your foot, and with the fingertips of one hand take the tip and apply enough pressure to make it arc slightly. Rotate the blank with your other hand. At some point, the blank will resist being rotated and then jump ahead. When this happens, the spine will be on the outward arc of the blank, away from your body. Again, you might not feel this reaction the first time. You should in any case rotate the blank through several turns, to be absolutely certain you're recognizing the resistance to turning and the springing ahead at the same point each time.

Method three is to hold the rod with widespread hands, one at the tip, the other well below the midpoint, and put the blank under gentle tension. Rotate by the tip. Again, there will be an instant when the blank seems reluctant or balky, doesn't want to rotate, and as you continue to rotate it, it will jump ahead. When this occurs, the spine is at the bottom of the blank's arc, away from you.

One method of finding a blank's spine: Rest the blade on a table edge or chair back a bit more than one-third down from the tip, and roll the tip between your fingertips. When the blank seems to resist rotation, then jumps ahead, the spine is at the *bottom* of the blank.

A second method of discovering the spinal line: Rest the blank's butt on your toe, as shown by Rich Miller; rotate the tip with your fingers until the balk-jump sequence occurs. When the sequence is most pronounced, the spinal plane is on the *outside curve* of the blank, away from you. Remember, all graphite blank makers warn against hand flexing of their blanks.

A third and final method of locating the spinal plane—but don't use it with graphite blanks. Hold the blade as shown, rotate the tip with your fingers of the upper hand. Again, the blank will seem to balk, then jump. This occurs when the spinal plane is on the *outside curve*, with a less apparent balk-jump sequence on the side opposite the spine.

Remember that when you buy a factory-ferruled blank and it is delivered unjointed, you must test each section to locate the spine. I'd apply this test routinely to all blanks, whether of fiberglass or graphite. Supposedly, graphite blanks have minimal spines because one of the final steps in their manufacture is to bind the longitudinal graphite fibers with a tape, applied in spirals, which shrinks when it is heated. But I've seen graphite blanks with pronounced spines, or strong sides. All tubular fiberglass rods have spines.

After finding the spine, which is a plane extending the length of the blank, mark it at tip, center, and butt. To align the spinal plane, tape a length of string to the mark at the tip, lay the blank flat and stretch the string taut, but not enough to flex the blank. Tape the string to the butt after you're sure it's in a direct line from the tip. Locating and marking the spine of a blank is a very important step; you'll refer to the spine markings many times.

Generally, you'll discover a blank's spine with the hand that's holding it by the tip. Mark it at once with a felt-tipped pen. Tie a length of string to the tip with the knot over the spine-mark and tape the other end to the butt. Mark the spine at any point where you'll be putting in a ferrule, as well as at the butt. The female half of a ferrule makes a good tool to hold the string in place while you mark the blank.

SETTING FERRULES

Here, we're going to look at the easiest way to fit a blank with both metal and glass-to-glass ferrules. Whichever you use, the job is quite straight-forward. You'll have no trouble if you work methodically and with reasonable care.

Begin with a clear, level space that gives you working room. This doesn't necessarily mean an area the size of a football field. Your workbench top or a tabletop is big enough for center measurements, but later you'll need a long level area; the concrete floor of a garage or basement is ideal.

Your first measurement is the outside diameter of the blank at the point where the ferrule will be fitted. This is always in 64ths of an inch, to correspond with the sizing of ferrules. You can use either of two methods, if you have neither a micrometer nor one of the ferrule gauges sold by Allan Tackle Manufacturing Co. through retail dealers. First, you can make a quite accurate gauge of medium-weight cardboard or light sheet metal by cutting a series of slots graduated in width from $^{10}/_{64}$ to $^{20}/_{64}$ inch, which are the midpoint blank diameters you'll most often encounter. Simply slip the slots over the blank until you find the one that fits.

To use the second method, you'll need either two carpenter's squares or framing squares, or one square and a straightedge. Hold or prop one square upright and put the blank in its corner. Slide the second square along the bottom of the first until it is firm against the blank, then read the blank's diameter from the bottom markings of the first square. If you use a straightedge instead of the second square, hold it upright pressed against the blank, and be sure the straightedge and the upright side of the square are parallel and the blank firmly held between them.

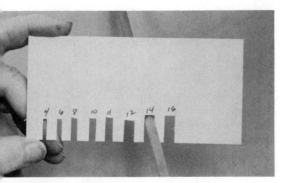

You can make a reasonably accurate gauge to measure the diameter of a blank by marking parallel lines at the edge of a piece of heavy cardboard, measuring in 64ths of an inch in any combination you wish, then cutting slots with a craft knife or razor blade.

For greater accuracy in measuring blank diameters for ferrules, use two squares as shown here, and measure the gap between the squares' upright sides with the rod held between them.

Setting ferrules is a job a lot of rod makers dread, but if you take the time to make a pattern or profile of your blank before you cut it, the job becomes very simple. Remember, your objective in setting ferrules is to keep the blank perfectly straight on both sides of the joint. Remember, too, that when held at one angle a ferrule joint can look straight, but when rotated a quarter- or half-turn it may be seen to be crooked when you sight along it. The lip of each ferrule must be at right angles to the blank around all 360° of its circumference, and if you've cut the blank at even a slight slant the ferrule may be thrown out of line by the cut end pressing on its bottom. A pattern or profile made before cutting will give you an exact reference to use later on.

To make the outline or profile of the blank that will be used later to determine whether you've set the ferrules straight, lay the blank on a clean board a bit longer than the blank itself. If you don't have such a board handy, attach a long strip of heavy wrapping paper to the floor with masking tape, making sure it is free from wrinkles. Use short strips of masking tape to keep the blank in place while you draw a line on each side parallel to the taper of the blank. It may help you to use a long straightedge a fraction of an inch from the sides of the blank to guide your pencil. The line can be as much as $\frac{1}{8}$ inch or a bit more from the sides of the blank. This outline or profile will be your guide later to make sure the ferrules are in exact alignment, so put the profile aside until later on.

Before cutting a blank to install ferrules, mark its profile on a board or long piece of wrapping paper. Tape the blank in place with masking tape, and use a straightedge to reproduce the blank's taper on the board or paper.

Separate the ferrule and put the male or plug half aside for the moment. Slide the female ferrule down the blank until it stops; this should be about 1 inch below the mark at the blank's midpoint. Mark around the blank at the bottom edge of the ferrule.

Remove the ferrule and lay it beside the blank, its bottom edge corresponding to the mark made when the ferrule was on the blank. Check to be sure that the centerline is about at the middle of the ferrule.

A moment's digression is called for here. We've been assuming that you're making a two-section rod ferruled in the center. If you happen to be making a three-section rod, you will of course have marked the blank off into equal thirds and will be doing your fitting at one of these points. The procedure is exactly the same, whether you're setting one ferrule or several. Before you can cut the blank, you must establish a point for each ferrule.

To return now to your two-section, center-ferruled rod making. Push

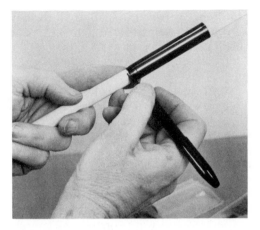

First step in measuring for your cut is to slip the female half of the ferrule over the blank and move it down to the point where it stops. Mark the point where its bottom edge occurs.

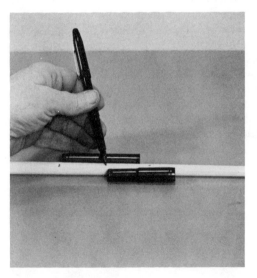

Lay the female half of the ferrule on one side of the blank with its bottom end at the mark made when it was on the blade. Lay the male half of the ferrule on the opposite side of the blank as above with its shoulder about ⅛ to ¼ inch below the top of the female half. Mark the point where the bottom of the male ferrule occurs. This mark is your cut line. (The mark above the male ferrule on the blank pictured is a spinal marking.) Move the male ferrule 1 to 1½ inches above the cut-line mark and make a second mark—your second cut line—removing the portion that will be taken up by the plug of the male ferrule when it's inserted.

the halves of the ferrule together, replace it by the rod with the bottom edge of the female ferrule in line with its stop-mark, and mark the blank at the top of the male ferrule. Pull the ferrule apart and put the male half in line with the mark you've just made. If the bottom of the plug is $^1/_2$ inch or less above or below the centerline mark, you're home free. If the distance is greater than $^1/_2$ inch either way, and you want a rod with sections that are exactly equal, you have two alternatives: lengthen the section that is too short, or shorten the section that is too long.

You can compensate quite easily for discrepancies between $^1/_4$ and $^1/_2$ inch. If the top section is too long, the blank can be trimmed a bit at the butt or the tip shortened. If the bottom section is too short, you can make up the difference with a butt cap or hosel; if it's too long, you can trim off a short piece. All these adjustments can be made without damage to the action of the finished rod. However, if the difference between the length of the sections is going to be $1/2$ inch or more, you'll be better advised to use a ferrule with an inside diameter $1/64$ inch smaller if you want it to fit higher on the butt section, or one with an ID $1/64$ inch larger if you want to set it lower on the butt.

To digress again, there's no law requiring a center-ferruled rod to have the ferrule *precisely* in the center. This is a purely cosmetic matter. I have several custom-made rods that vary as much as $1/2$ inch in section lengths, and when they're in use the difference isn't noticeable. If you take pride in your handwork, it's worth the trouble of getting a larger or smaller ferrule to make the sections come out exactly equal. But if you don't want to suspend work long enough to get a replacement ferrule, don't let a slight difference in section lengths bother you. If a friend notices it and asks you about it, just smile smugly and say nothing. He'll think you've discovered some deep secret that improves rod action and will probably put an off-center ferrule in the next rod he makes.

At this point you've made the necessary adjustments and marked a cut line on the blank, and are ready to cut it. Make a cutting jig by nailing two pieces of scrap lumber—a cove molding is ideal—on a board long enough to support the blank on both sides of the cut; nail these pieces 3 inches or so apart in the center of the supporting board. Push the blank against these blocks while you saw it. If you have no saw, use a file and rotate the blank under the edge of the file, scoring it a bit deeper with each turn. When the blank is parted into two pieces, smooth any ragged edges around the cut. This is also the time to square the edges if your cut's a bit uneven.

Cut the blank at the first cut line with a razor saw. See the text for details.

If you lack a razor saw, use a triangular file to cut the blank; rotate the blank against the file until it parts. A rest such as the one shown, made of scrap lumber, is a great help in keeping saw or file true, as well as in rotating the blank. Cutting with a file is slower than cutting with a razor saw, but it's better than risking a split blank by using a coarse saw blade.

Now, slip the female ferrule on the butt section of the blank. It should stop with its bottom edge on the mark you made when trying it on for size. Join the male portion of the ferrule to the female; if it seats all the way, you're home free. If it doesn't, that's a sign that the male ferrule is hitting the top of the blank, at the cut. Saw or file off about $1/16$ inch from the end, enough to allow the male ferrule to seat firmly in the female half.

Test the upper half of the blank in the male ferrule. If it doesn't slide to the bottom, or refuses to go into the barrel, sand the lower $1/2$ inch of the blank until you have a close fit. Work with the finest grade of sandpaper, rotating the area being sanded in the paper held in one hand, as shown. Use a light touch, take off only enough material to get a snug fit.

Due to the blank's taper, the upper portion of the female ferrule will probably fit loosely and wobble a bit. The traditional cure for this is to criss-cross a few spirals of thread on the top of the blank, just below the cut, but a more satisfactory method is to spread a very thin, even coating of epoxy on a 1-inch-wide strip of tissue paper and wrap the coated area smoothly around the blank just below the cut. You should need to make only three or four turns. When the epoxy hardens, sand the area until the female ferrule fits snugly on the blank. Cure looseness at the top of the male half of the ferrule in the same way.

When both cuts have been made, true up the ends of the blank by holding it vertical while rotating it on a piece of sandpaper resting on a flat surface, as shown. It's easier to get a square edge this way than it is by using a file or sanding block.

Before gluing the ferrules on, test for alignment. Join the ferrules on the blank, lay it on the profile you made at the beginning of the job, and rotate it slowly. Misalignment will be easy to spot. The tip will rise above the board or paper, and will also fall outside the profile. This indicates that one or both sections of the ferrule are fitted crookedly, and a crookedly set ferrule will throw a rod badly out of true.

Joint the male and female halves of the ferrule and slip the female end over the blank. If its edge reaches the mark you made at the beginning, you're home free. If it stops above the mark, that means the end of the male ferrule has hit the cut end. In this case you must saw or file off enough material to allow $\frac{1}{16}$- to $\frac{1}{8}$-inch clearance between the end of the blank and the end of the male ferrule plug.

There'll probably be enough looseness in the end of the blank—due to its taper—to cause the upper portion of the female ferrule to wobble. Mix a dab of epoxy and spread it on a strip of tissue paper (the gift-wrap, not the bathroom kind) and wrap this tightly over the top inch of the blank. When the epoxy sets up, sand for a push fit into the female ferrule.

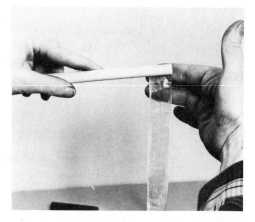

A slant of only a hair's thickness at the ferrule translates to an inch or more at the tip of the rod. Build up the low spot with short lengths of thread on the side of the blank where the ferrule slants off true. This is much more satisfactory than trying to sand the blank, especially if it's graphite. Neither fiberglass nor graphite blanks should be sanded beyond an essential minimum when you're setting ferrules on them.

It's a good idea to plug the ends of the blanks before gluing the ferrules in place. Plugs can be made from wood or cork, sanded to match the taper of the inner walls. Put the plug in the lower section of the blank from the butt end; apply adhesive to the inner wall rather than to the plug. Be sure to taper the ends of the plugs so they won't press in a line on the inner wall when the rod is flexed.

Now the ferrules can be set. If you've used thread to build up the diameter of either section, be sure it's soaked with adhesive. I've used most kinds of adhesives at one time or another, all the way from the sticks of ferrule cement and gasket shellac to the modern ones such as Pliobond and Featherweight's similar thermoplastic adhesive, and recommend either of the latter. They set up fairly slowly, which gives you time to cure any minor

Before gluing on the ferrules, joint them with the ends of the blank in place and test for straightness on the profile of the blank that you drew earlier. Rotate the jointed blank on the profile to discover misalignment shown.

misalignments of the ferrules, and can be softened by heat if a ferrule needs to be replaced.

Smear the ends of the blank with adhesive, and push the ferrules on. Wipe off excess glue, joint up the blank and test it on the profile to make sure that it's straight. At this point, you can cure minor misalignment by pressure on the ferrules. When the joint is absolutely true, lay it on a level surface that supports its entire length until the adhesive has set. Don't unjoint the rod, but let it rest jointed until the adhesive is completely dry.

That's the end of the job, except for one small but important detail. Mark the ferrules, both male and female, with a dot of enamel at the spine, so

As a final step before setting the ferrules permanently, plug the ends of the blank. Basswood pieces, sold by tackle shops as material from which casting lures can be made, work easily and are substantial. Avoid balsa, which is not strong enough. Cork is too soft.

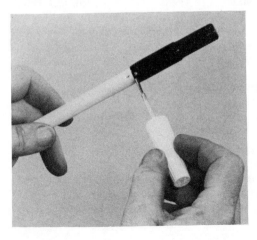

After the ferrules have been set, mark the spinal plane on them so the blank can be joined in correct alignment during later work, such as winding on the guides. Nail polish makes a mark that's easy to remove later on.

that when you take the blank apart for further work the spinal line can be relocated. Once the guides are set, of course, the sections will automatically be jointed in proper alignment.

Fitting a fiberglass blank with internal ferrules in no more difficult than setting metal ferrules, and the job takes about the same amount of time. DO NOT use this type of ferruling on graphite blanks, however. The fibers in graphite blanks are chiefly longitudinal and will eventually split because of the stresses resulting from internal ferruling. Some experts frown on using home-fitted internal ferrules on fiberglass blanks.

Gary Loomis, with whom I discussed this matter at some length, is production manager for Lamiglas, whose fiberglass rods have internal ferrules. Gary pointed out that Lamiglas ferrule plugs are computer-designed to match the flexing of the blanks on which they're fitted, and are hollow as well as flexible, while such ferrules put on in a home workshop are relatively rigid. Mike Stoker, of the California Tackle Co., also made this point about his firm's Sabre blanks, and added that these blanks have external support at the ferrule joint in the form of extra layers of fiberglass mesh.

A lot of amateur rod makers, myself among them, began fitting internal glass-to-glass ferrules several years ago, and I've heard of no problems from them, nor have I had any on my own rods. This doesn't mean that I discount the expert words of Gary or Mike, and I do recommend that you confine this style of ferruling to light-duty fly and spinning rods and reinforce the female joint, as will be explained later. Internal ferrules create about the same flat area that metal ferrules do, so in the final analysis I'll leave it up to your judgment whether or not you use them.

Start as with metal ferrule installation by profiling and dividing the blank, as already described and pictured. You'll need a piece from a solid fiberglass rod for the ferrule plug, which you can usually find for less than a dollar at a thrift shop or second-hand store. You might even have an old one knocking around the house that you'd be willing to sacrifice. Strip the solid glass rod of its fittings and give it a good wipe-down using household cleaner, detergent, or isopropyl alcohol.

If you can't find a used or broken solid fiberglass rod, shop discount stores or variety stores, which usually sell these rods new for less than $3.00. Solid fiberglass is really the most satisfactory material to use. Metal puts a weight at the wrong place in the rod and may chafe it internally, graphite is hard to work, and wood is too brittle. If you can't locate a solid fiberglass rod, look for a bike rod in a shop selling motorcycles or dune buggies. The bike rods used on these machines to hold flags high in the air are made of solid fiberglass. They're tubular, and you'll have to taper them with file and sandpaper to fit snugly into the rod blank you're ferruling, using the procedures that you'd use if you started with a pretapered section of solid fiberglass fishing rod.

Slip the solid rod into the butt of the new blank until it stops. Don't force it. Mark the solid rod at the point where it comes out of the tubular blank, remove it, and saw off the top and bottom, cutting 2 inches above and below the mark. This is your plug.

Coat the large end of the plug with pencil lead, or, better, with carpen-

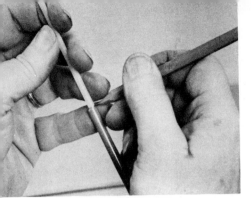

Fitting Glass Ferrules

1. When fitting a blank with glass-to-glass ferrules, after sawing the blank at the centerline, slide a section of an old solid fiberglass rod into the butt section. When it stops without being forced further, mark the solid glass rod at the end of the blank.

2. Mark the solid glass rod about 3 inches above and below the line at which it fits the blank's butt and saw at these two end lines. This piece forms the plug of your ferrule.

3. Coat the large end of the plug with pencil lead or carpenter's chalk, then rotate it in the butt section. Scraped places indicate high spots on the inner walls of the blank.

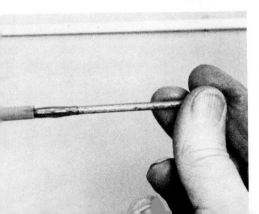

4. Use a long nail or piece of wire to coat the inner wall of the blank's butt section with epoxy. Don't put adhesive on the plug, for if you do the glue will be deposited on the inside of the blank as it's pushed into place.

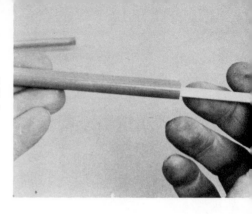

5. Push the plug into the butt section with a long dowel until it's seated firmly. Your next steps must wait until the epoxy has set completely, usually overnight.

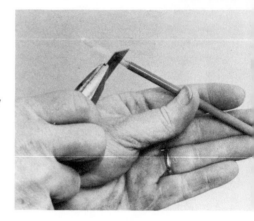

6. When the epoxy has set, scrape off any blobs it may have left on the ferrule plug.

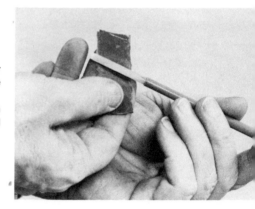

7. Light sanding with #400 auto body paper may be needed to get the final fitting of the plug in he upper section of the blank. Be sure the spinal planes are in line on both halves of the blank as you work out this final fitting.

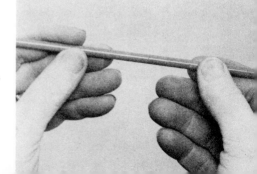

8. Your finished joint should be tight and almost invisible.

ter's chalk, the kind used in a chalk line. Drop the plug into the bottom end of the butt and push it gently with a long dowel until it stops, its end protruding from the blank. Hold the tip of the plug with your fingers and rotate it inside the blank, then remove it. Inspect the plug carefully for spots where the lead or chalk has not been rubbed off. If there are only a few, you have nothing to worry about; this shows the taper of the plug is a reasonably good match for the inner taper of the blank's wall.

If a lot of areas have been rubbed clean, sand the bottom of the plug lightly, test again after putting on a fresh chalk or pencil-lead coating. When the bottom of the plug is contacting all but a few spots around the blank's inner wall, you can repeat the process on the tip of the plug, fitting it into the upper section of the blank. You may have to smooth the inner wall of the blank's upper section with some #400 wet-or-dry body paper to get a smooth fit.

Put the plug back in the butt section of the blank and hold it with a dowel while you joint the upper section of the blank to it. Test the assembled blank on the profile, as when setting a metal ferrule, to be sure the blank is straight. You may have to sand one side of the plug or the other to get a perfectly straight blank when the spine marks on the lower and upper sections are in line.

Once you're sure the alignment of the blank is true, remove the upper section and mark the plug and the butt section with an overlapping line so they can be realigned while gluing. Mix a small quantity of epoxy and let it rest while taking the plug out of the blank. Apply the epoxy to the inside wall of the blank, using a long splinter or piece of dowel to be sure you're covering the entire area the plug will touch. Don't put the adhesive on the plug; it will make a glue line on the interior wall as it's placed, and this line might become a false spine and affect the rod's action.

Replace the plug in the butt section of the blank and seat it by pushing from the butt with a dowel. Line up the reference lines, then let the work rest until the epoxy is completely set. Scrape off any oozed-out glue at the point where the plug emerges, or any drops on its surface. Joint up the blank and test it on the profile again, being sure you joint it with the spine aligned. You should have a nice, straight blank on which to continue working.

Later, when winding the blank, you'll reinforce the rims of both butt and tip sections, but this will be done only after you've fitted grip, reel seat, and guides.

FORMING AND FITTING GRIPS

Sooner or later you're going to be faced with the job of forming a cork grip from scratch, if you do any amount of rod making at all, so this job is going to be our starting point. Because the grip and reel seat are usually a unit, we'll associate them here, just as you'd do when working on a rod blank.

There's a difference only of length and contour between the grips of any rod, baitcast/spincast, spinning, fly, or whatever. The method of forming them from scratch is the same. In later chapters, where specific details about forming grips for different kinds of rods are discussed, you'll find

After transferring a template pattern to a piece of stiff cardboard as detailed in the text, cut the template with a craft knife to make a profile of the grip you're going to form.

templates that will help you form the contours and some suggestions about the lengths and diameters of grips for rods of various types.

Templates in the illustrations are all reduced in size, so your first job will be to enlarge them. Draw 1-inch squares on a piece of stiff cardboard to guide you in transferring the curves from the illustrations to your full-scale template. If you have a draftsman's French curve, it will help in getting the contours smooth, but there are a lot of substitutes for it: a big platter or tray or the lid of a roasting pan can provide gentle curves that will guide your pencil. After you've drawn the contour line, cut along it with a sharp knife. The template's inside contour gives you the outside contour of the grip. By holding the template to the cork as you're filing or sanding it, and rotating the partly formed grip against the template edge, you can get a perfectly shaped grip with the same contour all the way around.

For our prototype grip, let's choose a lightweight fly rod. You'll need 14 cork rings to form such a grip. These rings are uniformly $1/2$ inch thick, but are made in a variety of inside and outside diameters. Inside diameters are $1/4$, $3/8$, and $1/2$ inch; outside diameters are 1, $1^1/8$, $1^1/4$, and $1^1/2$ inches. You can get several combinations of inside and outside diameters, $1/4$-inch ID and $1^1/2$-inch OD, $1/2$-inch ID and 1-inch OD, and so on. Choose an inside diameter a bit smaller than the outside diameter of the blank being fitted and an outside diameter that will allow you to remove at least $1/8$ inch of material in forming the grip's biggest bulge.

Let's assume we're fitting a grip to a blank with a .500 (or $1/2$-inch) outside diameter at the butt. Typically, you'll encounter less than $1/4$ inch of taper from the bottom of the blank to the point at which the grip ends, so you'll use $3/8$-inch ID rings. If the butt tapers extremely fast, you might begin with $3/8$ inch and shift at midpoint to $1/2$-inch ID rings. Often you can save a bit of work by using rings of a smaller outside diameter where the grip tapers inward.

Allow two rings for each inch of grip. Number all the rings in sequence, and on one side of each mark a right-angle cross. This is your reference when you're reaming. Ream with a rattail file, turning the ring a quarter-turn between each three or four file strokes to keep the inside diameter

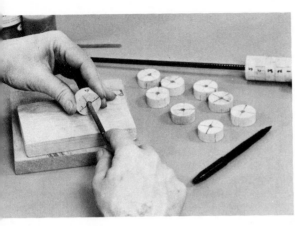

Mark cork rings with a right-angle cross and number each ring; the cross-mark is your reaming guide. Start on one line and rotate the cork after each three or four strokes of your rat-tail file to keep the center hole concentric. The size of the center hole will diminish as the blank tapers, so each ring must go on the blank in sequence.

uniform. As you ream, test each ring for fit on the blank; you want a snug but not a tight fit. Be sure to allow for the length of the reel seat; the grip should start 4 inches above the very bottom of the blank. If you wish, you can glue on the reel-seat bushings and reel seat before starting to form the grip.

A word of caution here: If you're working on a graphite blank that has its female ferrule on the butt section, be sure to check its diameter at both top and bottom. On some lightweight graphite blanks, the diameter of the ferrule sleeve is greater than the diameter of the butt. This means you must build your grip from the top ring down. Such rods as this taper very little at the butt, and you should have no problem doing this.

To revert to reel-seat bushings. These come in a variety of outside diameters, $^3/_8$, $^1/_2$, and $^9/_{16}$ inch, while inside diameters are $^3/_4$, $^{13}/_{16}$, and $^{15}/_{16}$ inch. As in the case of cork rings, several combinations of inside/outside diameters enable you to match the blank's outside diameter with the inner diameter of the reel seat. Bushings may be made of cork, paper, or wood; cork is easiest to work, but all materials are satisfactory. They are worked like cork rings, reamed inside to fit the blank and filed or sanded to match the reel seat's inside diameter.

After you've done the reaming and fitting, you have two options in gluing and forming the grip. One is to glue the grip on the rod and form it there; the other is to glue the grip-rings on a length of threaded rod and form them in a drill. Both methods take about the same length of time.

If you choose to work directly on the blank, you'll need in addition to the corks and reel-seat bushings some kind of waterproof glue, some sturdy rubber bands, and a piece of plywood of any thickness, about $1^1/_2$ to 2 inches square.

Spread glue on the butt of the blank up to the point where the grip will end. Rest the blank on the plywood—cover the wood with waxed paper to keep it from getting stuck to the work—and slide on the reel-seat bushings in sequence, gluing them at the edges. Begin putting on the rings in sequence, spreading a coat of adhesive on the top of each. Don't put glue on the top of the final ring, of course. You can either put on the reel seat at

When all the rings have been fitted, coat the center hole and
top surface of each cork in turn
and slide it on the blank. If you
are forming a fly-rod grip, put
on the reel-seat bushings later;
spinning-rod grips with the reel
seat between butt and foregrips
must have the bushings and
reel seat fitted as the corks are
added.

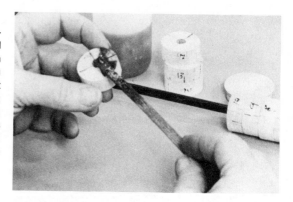

When all corks are glued in
place, use a small scrap of
plywood and rubber bands cut
from an old innertube to make
a pressure clamp to hold the
cork rings while the glue dries.

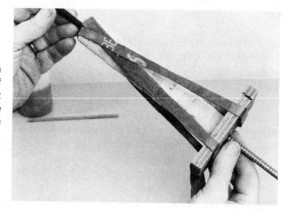

A more effective clamp can be
made from two pieces of scrap
plywood drilled to accept
lengths of threaded rod stock.
The picture shows the details
of this clamp.

this point, or fit it later. When you do set it, be sure its fixed hood is in line
with the blank's spine.

When all the rings are on the blank, slip a rubber band under the
plywood square and bring it up over the top ring. Put on the second rubber
band, crisscrossing it with the first as shown in the picture. Set the grip
aside to let the work dry thoroughly before starting to form the grip to contour. Most waterproof adhesives require 24 to 48 hours before they're
hard.

Another digression. If you're going to make more than one rod, forget about rubber bands. Make a gluing clamp from two pieces of thick plywood about 4 inches square. Drill both pieces about $3/4$ inch in from the edge on opposite sides, using a $5/8$-inch bit. Drill one piece of the plywood in the center with a $1/2$-inch bit. Put lengths of $1/4$-inch threaded rod through the matched holes on the sides; countersink one piece of the plywood or nail slats to its bottom so it will stand upright when the nuts on each end of the threaded rod are in place. When your grip is glued up, slip the piece of plywood with the center hole over the end of the blank, put the butt on the other piece, and tighten the nuts on top of the plywood to press the cork rings together. The picture will give you the details needed to make this handy press.

When the glue is dry and out of the press, protect the reel seat and the blank with masking tape before you start forming the grip. Begin by marking the grip with lines 90° apart along its length. Carry the lines down the butt of the grip, and make small marks between them to give you reference points as to the grip's diameter, so you won't take off too much material.

First, square the grip with a mill bastard file. When the cork is squared, file away the corners to form an octagon. From that point it's a simple matter to round the rings. Then, form the contour of the grip, using a template to guide you. When the contours have been roughed in, switch to coarse sandpaper—about a #39 or #40 garnet cabinet paper makes a quick job of the final rough-in and won't tear up the cork as badly as a file or rasp.

Rotate the blank with one hand while holding the paper in a U-shape in the other hand. Never sand up and down the length of the blank with anything but a fine finishing sandpaper, unless you're trying to form an oval grip. Always work around, and always keep both blank and sandpaper in motion to avoid taking off too much surface material in one spot.

When your template shows that the grip is nearing its finished form, begin using #80 sandpaper, and in the final stage of forming, switch to #120 paper. For final polishing, go to #400 auto body finishing wet-or-dry paper, using it wet. This puts the final smooth finish on cork. Even the best species of cork available today will have pits in it. These can be filled with some adhesive in which dust from the final sanding has been mixed, and the patches allowed to dry hard before smoothing them with #120 sandpaper followed by a final polishing. Pits and blemishes can also be filled with a product called FI:X Wood Patch; it's waterproof and doesn't shrink as it hardens. It sets quite rapidly, so work fast if you use it.

Except for the difference in contours, spinning rod grips can be formed on the blank by the procedures just detailed. The only difference is that you'll place the reel seat between a foregrip and butt grip, and seat and bushings must be set while you're gluing up the cork rings. The reel seat can be protected with masking tape while you're working. The hosel or butt cap should be fitted before you start forming the grip.

Quite honestly, I prefer to form grips in a drill and then fit them to the blank. Maybe this is because I learned the drill method before the one just described. Here's how you proceed if you have an electric drill that you can

Begin the forming by marking the cork rings with four lines 90° apart. Hold your straightedge in line with the center of the blank when marking. Notice that the grip being marked in the picture has two top rings of smaller outside diameter than those in the body of the grip; this reduces the amount of filing to be done.

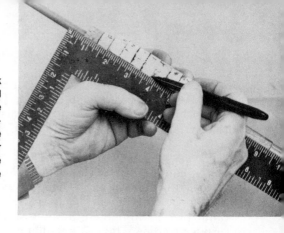

Your first file cut squares off one side of the corks between two of the horizontal lines.

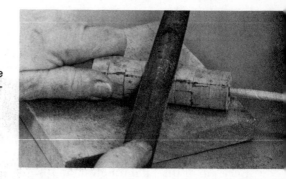

From the end, the grip should look like this after the first filing has been done. Small marks on the bottom will help you judge the depth of cuts when filing. Square the corks by filing them flat between the four lines, then file flats along the corners of the corks to give the grip an octagonal shape.

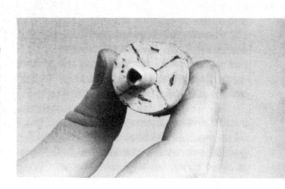

Now, it's easy to round the octagon into a circle. Notice that your file cuts have been straight, forming the corks into a cylinder. Don't try to form the contours during the first steps of forming. On blanks where the reel seat has been fitted before the grip is filed, protect the reel seat and the few inches of blank above the grip with masking tape, as shown.

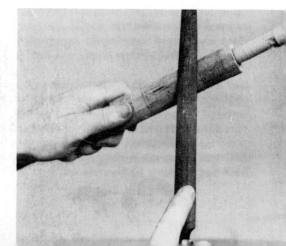

48

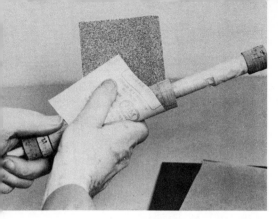

Use coarse sandpaper held as shown to finish rounding the corks and start forming the grip's contours. Rotate the grip against the paper rather than trying to sand up and down.

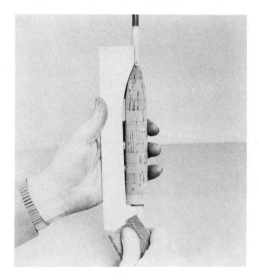

Check progress of sanding with the template. The grip being formed in the picture needs to be reduced by sanding the two or three top rings so the edge of the template will extend to the center of the blank. Switch at this point to a finer grade of sandpaper and begin giving the cork its final smooth finish.

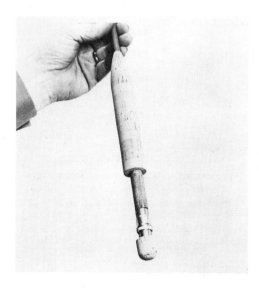

Do your final sanding with #400 wet-or-dry auto body paper used wet to give the cork its final polish. The completed grip should look like this.

mount in a vise or in one of the stands made to hold hand drills horizontally, or if you have a vertical drill press.

You'll need a piece of threaded rod $\frac{1}{4}$ inch in diameter, two washers and two nuts for each end of the rod, and some masking tape. Fit the rings to the blank as described earlier, but do not glue them to the blank or to each other. Run a nut about $1\frac{1}{2}$ inches up on one end of the threaded rod, then run up the second nut and tighten it against the first. This will prevent the nuts from working loose when the rod is spinning in the drill. Wrap masking tape around the rod about $\frac{1}{2}$ inch above the washer to form a bushing that will keep the corks centered on the rod. If the grip you're forming is short, make another masking-tape bushing where the grip's center will be on the rod, and a third at the top. For long grips, you may have to form four or five bushings.

Now, proceed to build up the rings on the threaded rod just as you did on the blank, as described earlier, with a coating of glue on the upper surface of each ring. Omit the reel-seat bushings, put all the grip rings on the rod, then the washer and nut, finally the locknut. Use a wrench to draw up the first nut until the rings are in firm contact. If they slip out of place, align them with a piece of waxed paper over your hand to keep it from contact with the glue. Set the glued, clamped rings aside and let the glue dry bone-hard.

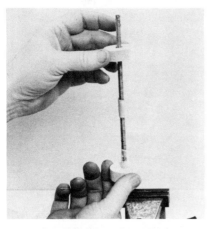

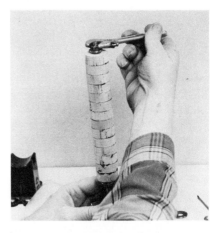

To form a grip in a drill on a length of threaded rod, begin by reaming the cork rings as shown earlier to fit the blank's butt taper. Fix the threaded rod upright in a vise or clamp with washers and a locknut at the bottom. Form bushings around the threaded rod at top, middle, and bottom, using masking tape; cover the tape with a strip of waxed paper to keep glue from sticking to it. Put the cork rings on in sequence, after coating their top sides with glue.

When all the corks are in place, put on a washer or two and a locknut and tighten the nut until the cork rings are firmly pressed together. Keep the rings centered while tightening, protecting your hands with a piece of waxed paper while pressing them into concentricity. They will try to slide around a bit as the nut works down.

When the glue has set, chuck one end of the rod into the drill, which should be held firmly in a vise or stand as shown in the pictures. Use the mill bastard file to rough in the contours, and switch to the smooth-cut file when roughing-in is complete. For fast cutting, use the file against the direction of the drill's revolution; for slow cutting, use it with the revolution of the work. Use a template often, stopping the drill and rotating it by hand against the template, to be sure you're holding to the contour you're after.

You can form both butt grip and foregrip for a spinning rod at once, by putting a cardboard or metal foil spacer between the two; just remember not to glue the two grips together when putting the rings on the rod.

Finish off with successively finer grades of sandpaper, used in strips as illustrated, and polish with wet-or-dry auto body paper as described earlier. If there are pits in the cork, gather a spoonful of the finest cork sanding dust left under the work, mix it with a few drops of Pliobond, and use the paste to fill the pitted spots before giving the grip its final polish.

Coat the butt of the rod with waterproof glue or Pliobond and slip on the butt grip, reel-seat bushings, reel seat—remembering as mentioned earlier to align the reel-seat hood with the blank's spine—and the foregrip. Clamp the grip in place with rubber bands or the gluing jig as described earlier and wait for it to dry before winding the guides on the blank.

There are several variations that you can consider in forming cork grips. One is buying preformed grips, which need only to be reamed to match the blank's taper and glued in place. They are available in tapered bores or straight bores. Most tackle houses that deal in rod-making materials have these grips, but the number of shapes is limited, and not all the preformed grips can be worked down to suit your own wishes. You can save time by buying glued-up cork rings, called sticks. These come in the same inside and outside diameters as the rings. You can also buy foam plastic grips to fit most blanks; these need only to be slipped into place on the blank's glue-covered butt. You'll encounter all these options in later chapters.

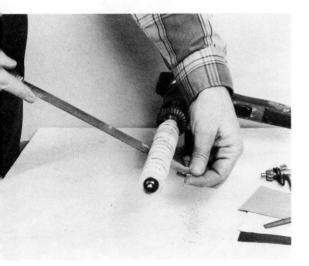

Use a drill stand such as the one shown at left in the previous picture, or chuck the handle of the drill in a vise to hold it in a horizontal position. Start forming the grip with a coarse file such as the half-round mill bastard shown. Don't start with a rasp, or you'll tear up the corks.

When the grip is roughed in, switch to coarse sandpaper, held in a strip as shown. Rather than concentrating on one spot, work along the entire length of the grip, using heavy and light pressure as required to shape the contour.

Switch to medium grits sooner than you think you need to, or you risk removing too much material. Use the template often, stopping the drill while you check the grip's contour.

When the grip is fully formed, polish it with #400 wet-or-dry auto body paper used wet. Work with narrow strips of sandpaper instead of big sheets.

Fill pits in the grip with a cork paste made as described in the text, or use a plastic wood filler. When the filler dries, smooth the grip with fine sandpaper and return to the threaded rod and drill for a final polishing with wet #400 auto body paper.

To finish the grip, use either a cork button, which you can make from a solid cork of the kind used in vacuum bottles, or you can use a plastic or metal butt cap or a hosel. Be sure to allow for the length of the butt cap when planning where to cut the blank, or trim off the butt to accommodate the kind of cap used.

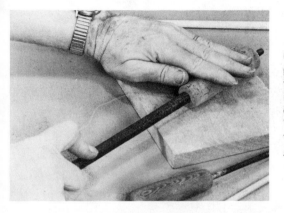

Use rattail files for reaming short preformed cork grips or grips made from glued-up cork sticks. File as you roll the grip slowly along the surface of the workbench or a block of wood. With a bit of practice you can match the taper of a blank by slanting the file just a slight amount.

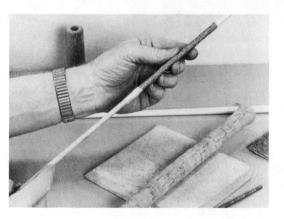

To ream long grips, those so long that your files won't span their length, wrap coarse sandpaper strips around a dowel, holding the ends of the paper with masking tape.

Use the sandpaper-covered dowel just as you would a file, rolling the grip smoothly over a flat surface.

Check progress of the reaming often. The marks on the butt of the blank above show where the bottom of the grip stopped after a series of reamings. If you suspect there are high spots on the grip's bore, rub lead pencil or carpenter's chalk over the blank when testing the grip for bore size; rubbed places reveal uneven inner spots that can be smoothed out with spot reaming.

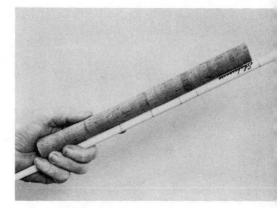

Fly-rod cork skeleton reel seats and many spinning-rod grips must be finished off with a cork button to close the butt. Make these with a file from big vacuum bottle or medicine jar stoppers, left, or from grip rings and cork bass-bug bodies, right. The bass-bug body is reduced to fit the hole in a cork ring, glued in place, and the upper half filed to match the inside taper of the blank.

If you use a cork button, sand and file the cork to match the diameter of the grip, leaving a plug at the top by which to glue it to the inner wall of the blank. If you use a butt cap, file and sand the bottom ring or rings to its inside diameter and glue the cap in place. Some metal butt caps must be screwed into a plug of wood fitted into the butt of the blank and glued in place. Hosels are usually made with a center hole that accommodates a dowel glued into the plug that closes the butt of the blank.

If you have a hole saw for your drill, you can cut rings for hosels with it from thin pieces of hardwood of contrasting tones, such as walnut and maple, or you can use a single kind of hardwood and cut contrasting disks from sheets of plastic. Taper the hosel by using the threaded rod on which you formed the grip, filing or sanding it to contour.

You can make a wooden-barreled reel seat if you want to add another custom touch to your rod. Simply drill a section of dowel the required length and diameter and ream it to the taper of the blank. Cut off the fixed hood and locking ring assembly from a metal reel seat and glue them with Pliobond to opposite ends of the dowel, which can be stained any shade you wish and varnished. Or, form a wooden cylinder of contrasting wooden rings, as in making a hosel, and attach the reel-seat hood and ring assembly to it.

There's one more thing you can do to personalize your rod in a way that

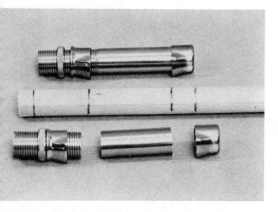

Here are the components for a wooden center reel seat. The metal reel seat at top is sawed off at the bottom of the locking nut thread and just above the fixed hood. The dowel—walnut, maple, or ash—is reduced by filing to accept threaded section and hood. It is then center-bored and reamed to fit the butt of the blank. Screw thread and hood are glued in place with waterproof glue or epoxy.

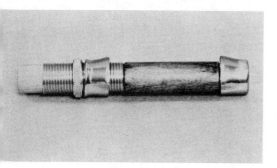

After gluing, the excess length of dowel is sawed off and the end filed smooth. The center of the reel seat is stained and varnished. Cork reel seats are made in this same manner.

will make it easily identifiable. Put your thumbprint on the grip. This trick was passed on to me many years ago by Jack Cuthrell, a good fishing companion who shared my interest in making rods as well as using them.

After you've established the spot on the grip where your thumb normally rests while you're casting, use a rattail or half-round file to form an oval depression in the grip at that point. Fill the cavity with fine-grained wood filler paste, and dip your thumb in fine, light oil. Press your thumb into the filler paste, holding the grip in your hand as you do while casting. Keep the thumb motionless for the ten or fifteen seconds required for the paste to begin setting up, then lift it straight up and out. This leaves your thumbprint on the paste. When dry, sand or file the grip to remove the

To personalize a rod grip with your own thumbprint, use a half-round file to form an oval recess near the top of the grip (*continued*).

Spread a thick coat of wood paste in the hollow oval. Wait a few seconds for the wood paste to begin setting up.

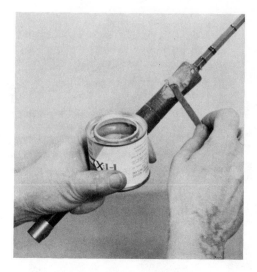

Hold the grip with your hand in casting position and press your thumb—coated with light cooking oil—firmly into the wood paste. Hold the thumb in place without moving it for 15 to 20 seconds. The oil keeps the wood paste from sticking to your skin.

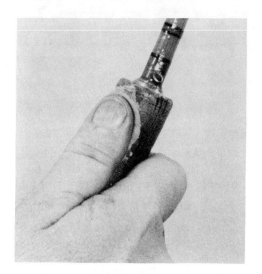

ragged edges of the filler. Nobody's going to argue the ownership of a rod that's been personalized in this fashion.

As mentioned earlier, forming grips for different types of rods involves basically the same procedures for all freshwater and most saltwater rods. We'll cover them in detail in the appropriate chapters, where you'll also find templates to use in shaping grips to various contours.

GUIDES AND TIPTOPS

Even the best guides will often have some slight irregularities on the bottoms of their feet. The irregularity usually takes the form of a tiny ridge down the center of the foot, and this must be removed before the guide is fitted to the blank. Use a smooth file or whetstone as illustrated, keeping the bottom of the feet flat on the abrasive surface, and rub the feet back and forth until they are perfectly smooth.

Then, help your winding job go more smoothly by tapering the feet to a finer edge than is possible in the manufacturing process. Use the file or stone for this, too. Don't try for a knife-edge that may cut the winding thread, just a gentler taper than the feet have in their original condition. Winding, which will be detailed later on, will be greatly simplified if you do this little bit of handwork in advance.

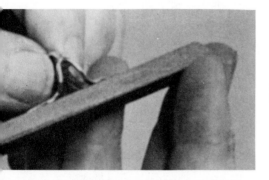

A small hook hone is ideal for smoothing the feet of guides.

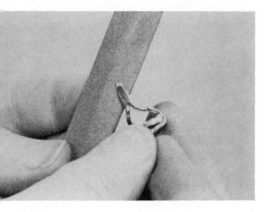

Use the hone also to taper the tips and sides of the guide feet.

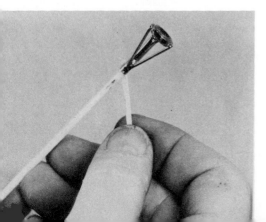

When fitting a tiptop on a blank, use a toothpick to make a tapered ramp of adhesive from the blank to the rim of the tiptop's barrel; this will ease the job of winding later on.

Tiptops are sized in 64ths of an inch, the measurement being that of the barrel's inside diameter. Most blanks are molded to a dimension onto which a tiptop of the correct size will slide smoothly. Occasionally, you'll find a blank that won't accept the tiptop it should, and in this case go to one a 64th larger in preference to sanding the delicate tip. Use epoxy-soaked tissue paper to build up the tip of the blank to get a snug fit. Be sure the epoxy is hard before sanding when you set the tiptop.

Using an oversized tiptop will leave a gap that winding thread can't climb smoothly. Form a miniature ramp with the adhesive, using a toothpick for a tool, as illustrated. When the adhesive is dry, you may have to sand lightly to smooth it, but it'll make winding in the tiptop a lot easier.

WINDINGS

This section includes winding materials and methods as well as the fitting of guides and tiptops. It doesn't go into the details of spacing and choosing guides; these are included in the chapters that follow dealing with specific types of rods. We're concerned here with basic techniques that apply to the majority of winding jobs you'll encounter, but such special ones as double- and triple-winding saltwater rods will be found in the chapters devoted to saltwater tackle. The material that follows will see you through most fresh-water rods.

In Chapter 2, winding rests were illustrated and explained, as were methods of winding without a rest. Using a rest makes most winding easier, but you can wind freehand, using a fly-tying bobbin to control the thread, or maintaining thread tension by putting the spool in a small jar or glass and passing the thread through a heavy book. Both are shown here. If you use the book method, select some volume such as an outdated telephone directory, not a valued book, for the winding thread will cut a slash through a page or two at some time or other, no matter how carefully you work.

You really must discover for yourself which method of thread tension control suits you best, just as you must select the shades of color you will use on a given rod. In Chapter 2, three types of winding rests were pictured, any of which can be made in a half-hour or so. Similar rests can be bought from Orvis and Herter, and most tackle shops have the metal Thompson rest in stock.

There are two basic techniques you need to learn from the start. These are the methods of beginning and finishing any winding. Both are pictured, and the illustrations demonstrate them better than a dozen paragraphs of text.

Windings on rods fall into two categories: functional and ornamental. The functional windings are those which hold guides in place, and close tiny gaps such as the hairline cracks between grip and rod; ornamental windings include trim strips and fancy butt winds. Sometimes the two become one; for instance, the winding above the grip not only closes a gap, but usually extends up the rod in a spiral or diamond pattern, and into it a hook keeper is usually incorporated on fly and spinning rods.

When winding on guides, your functional thread should start and end between six and ten turns from the foot of the guide; a trim strip above and

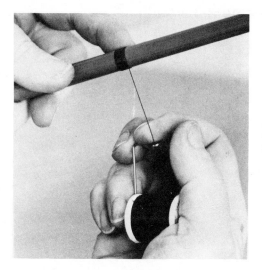

Many rod makers who also tie flies wind rods freehand, using a tying bobbin to control thread tension.

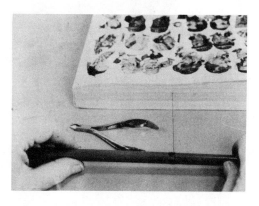

The standard way of winding a blank without a rest is to use a book to maintain thread tension. Keep the spools in a small jar behind the book, and use other books at right and left of your hands to hold the blank at working height above the bench top.

below each foot-winding is optional, as is a spiral under the guide itself. If you feel better with a marked and measured limit on each foot, by all means measure, using the center ring of the guide as your point of reference. Generally, the number of turns beyond the tip of a guide's foot increases as the diameter of the blank decreases. The very practical reason for this is that the winding thread is held in place solely by the tension of the few turns taken on the under-wound end when the wind started and by that created on the opposite end when the thread was pulled under itself. As the blank tapers to its point, more over-winding turns are necessary to keep the end under tension, and more turns should be taken around the pull-loop when finishing the wind.

Thread diameter also plays a part in determining how much you should over-wind and pull under. The small-diameter threads, 00 and A, will hold with fewer turns than will those in sizes D, E, and EE; the smaller diameters actually bring more pressure to bear per fraction of a linear inch than do

Basic Ornamental Winding

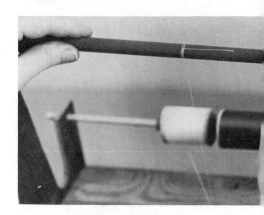

1. All windings are started the same way. Make one turn with the thread overlapping itself *in the direction of the wind.* Hold the overlapped X in place while winding two or three more turns over the end of the thread.

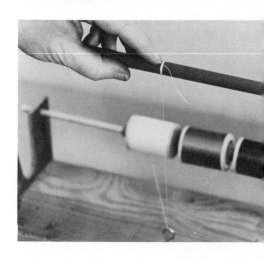

2. Push the thread together and true it up with a fingernail while maintaining tension on the winding. Trim the loose thread end.

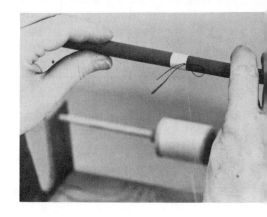

3. Rotate the rod to add additional courses of thread, keeping its tension uniform, until you're within five or six turns of the point where the winding will end. Wrap the winding thread over a loop of thread, the closed end of the loop at the outside of the wrapping.

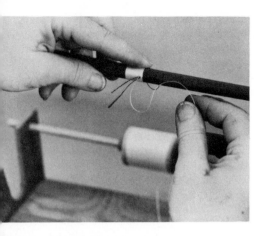

4. Holding the winding firm with one finger, cut the winding thread and pass its end through the loop.

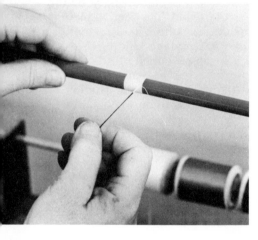

5. With a single smooth tug, pull the ends of the loop to carry the end of the winding thread under the winding.

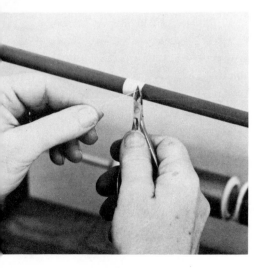

6. Keep a gentle tension on the loose end of the excess winding thread while you clip it off flush with the wind, using cuticle nippers. Finally, use a fingernail to smooth and align the ends of the winding, and to close any voids or gaps between courses of the winding thread.

the big diameters, because they flatten out when tightened, while the big threads touch the rod's surface with only a portion of their circumference. A rule of thumb to observe when winding is therefore: the smaller the thread diameter, the fewer anchoring turns will be required.

Let's get back to our guide winding now by doing a bit of backtracking. The pictures illustrating the winding-on of guides show the guides being held in place with masking tape, put there when the guides were spaced or positioned on the blank. This matter of guide spacing is covered in later chapters, because the placement of a rod's guides varies according to each individual type of rod and may vary somewhat with identical blanks from the same maker. The method of winding guides on, however, varies only marginally between types of guides, whether you're setting snake guides on a fly rod or big ring guides on a spinning rod. At this point, then, just assume that you've spaced the guides on the blank and are starting to wind them on.

In the accompanying pictures, the easiest way of starting your thread over the toe of the guide's foot is shown in detail. The feet, as mentioned earlier, will have been honed to a smooth, flat bottom and the toes or tips tapered to a fine edge. This makes it easy to spiral the winding thread over the foot and push it into place without having it bunch up.

This technique, by the way, won't work on guides that have grooves on the tops of their feet. These grooves are intended to make winding easier but actually make it more difficult. The best thing to do when you're faced with winding surface-grooved guides is to hone the grooves away when you're tapering the feet. Nothing in the way of strength is sacrificed, since the feet of most guides have quite a bit of excess metal in them.

Winding On a Guide

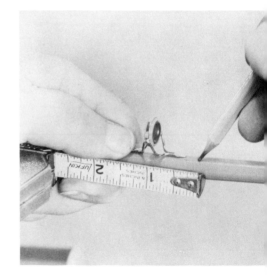

1. With a little practice, you'll be able to judge winding widths by eye, but for safety, measure winding distances from the ring of ring guides and the top curve of snake guides. Mark the blank at the point where the winding will begin and end.

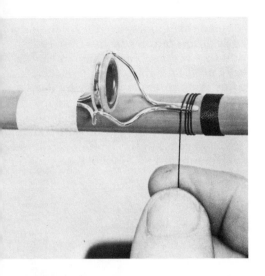

2. Don't spin your wheels trying to make the winding thread climb the toe of the guide. Instead, spiral it up a fraction of an inch above the toe and take three or four turns, as illustrated.

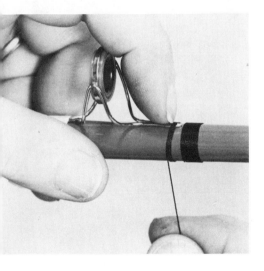

3. Maintain tension on the winding thread while pushing the spiraled courses down to and over the toe of the guide.

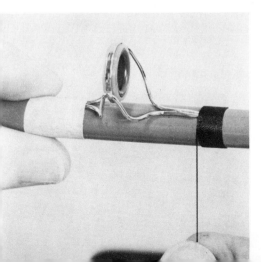

4. Then, continue to wind in close turns until you reach the end of the guide's foot, where the thread is cut and pulled under with a loop as already shown.

Many makers of graphite rods recommend that guides be under-wound on heavy-duty rods; under-winding simply means putting down a course of thread along the area where the guide's feet will go. The accompanying photos show how this is done; they really need no explanation here.

As for the spiral decorative wind, this is quite easily put on by eye, though if you're unsure of your judgment in spacing the spiral's loops, measure and mark the blank with a tiny pencil dot that the thread will hide.

There are a few specialized methods of guide winding, used on saltwater rods, which we'll deal with in later chapters devoted to this kind of tackle. Let's turn our attention now to the ornamental kind of windings.

Some guides are set on an under-wound course of winding thread rather than directly on the blank. Many makers of graphite rods recommend this method of fitting. Lay down the underwinding; it can be in individual winds for each guide foot, solid from end to end, or spaced under the guide ring with a spiral as illustrated. Mark the spot at which the overwinding starts and ends.

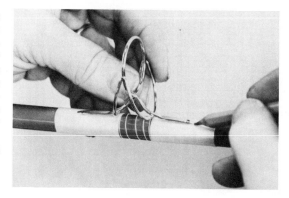

Winding the underwinding and guide wind in contrasting or complementary colors provides a trim strip at each end of each winding. The winding pictured in progress above will end at the guide's braces, then the other foot will be wound separately in the same manner.

Spiral decorative windings can be spaced by eye, or the blank can be measured and marked with spacings.

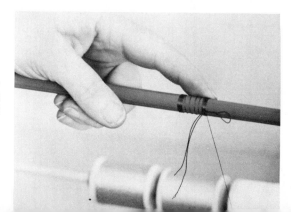

Two of the most common of these are the two-toned trim wrap that may be placed between the butt and first guide, or even between guides along the rod's length. The two-toned wrap is also used on many rods to dress up ferrule windings and in many cases, guide windings. On some rods, guides are wound with a central or primary color between trim strips of a contrasting or complementary shade of thread. Fancy jobs may include a central spiral under the guide ring or at the ends of the winding.

If you're thinking in terms of a very narrow trim strip, you have two options. One is to use Gudebrod's Space Dye thread, which has equally long segments of different colors. Simply trim the ends of the thread to the length required to form the trim strip, and the second color follows automatically. The length of each segment is 18 inches, and my experience with this thread indicates that you should trim from 6 to 8 inches from each succeeding segment as you go up the blank's taper to make your trim colors come out right.

There's another way to add a very narrow trim strip to a winding. It takes a bit of practice to master but is a very useful wind to know about. It works best with fine thread, 00 or A. To make the wrap, tie in your trim color thread with two firm turns, and on the opposite side of the blade, anchor the primary color thread with two more turns. Use the primary thread to anchor the trim thread and cut the trim thread after two anchoring turns. Wind the primary thread the desired number of turns, and when you are four to five turns away from finishing the primary winding, anchor the trim thread with the primary thread. Use the trim thread to tie off the primary thread, and place the pull-loop in position after two turns of the trim thread have been wound on, pull the end of the trim thread under to finish the winding job.

If this sounds confusing, the pictures should clarify things for you. Just remember that you must perform the anchoring and tying-off within a turn of one another. It takes a bit of practice, but the man I learned this from, E. C. "Pop" Powell, had practiced enough to be a master of threads. It was his habit to put one or two trim strips only three or four threads wide on the butt sections of his fine bamboo rods.

While we're on the subject of trim windings, let me go on record as favoring the delicate trim rather than the ornate kind that looks like embroidery on a pillowcase or tablecloth. There is a practical reason for this. The overlong, extra-fancy windings seen on some rods can very definitely affect the rod's action, the effect being greater on light fly and spinning rods than on baitcast/spincast or other husky rods. Whenever you clutter up a blank with excessive quantities of winding thread at any point higher than 12 to 14 inches above the grip, you run the risk of creating the same kind of flat spot as that created by a ferrule.

There is, of course, less danger of doing this on heavy-duty rods than on light ones. On heavy surf and trolling rods you can lay on the windings with a lavish hand. Naturally, it's up to you to decide whether you want to make rods that are pretty to look at but are likely to perform less satisfactorily because they're inhibited by yards upon yards of winding thread looped tightly around them, often layer upon layer.

Winding Trim Strips

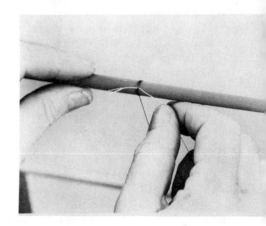

1. Very narrow-banded trim strips must be wound as a unit, because at least three turns of size A thread are required to anchor when winding in a thread; bigger sizes take a larger number of turns. Begin with a two-thread locking turn to anchor the first trim thread and with the third and fourth turns anchor the primary thread.

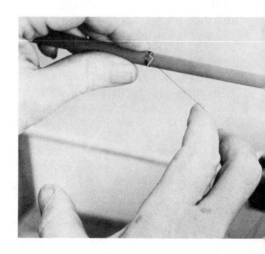

2. Use the first two turns of the primary thread to anchor the trim thread.

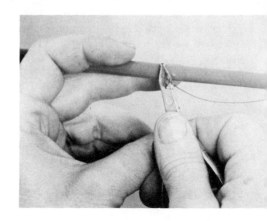

3. Cut the trim thread after the third turn of the primary thread.

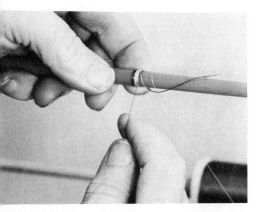

4. Anchor the trim thread for the finishing band with the fifth and sixth turns of the primary thread, cross the trim thread over the primary thread at once and anchor off the primary thread with two turns and cut it.

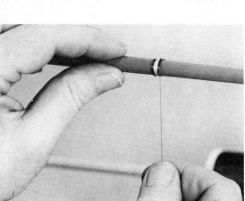

5. On the next turn of the second trim band thread, wind the pull-loop in. (This is the point at which the winding above is shown.) Take two turns with the second trim band thread and pull the end under in the usual manner. Remember, very narrow bands can be wound only with fine threads.

Look at the rods created by such master craftsmen of the past as Gillum, Payne, Young, Orvis, Leonard, Powell, Winston, and others. You'll be struck by their simplicity. While most of these men put narrow trim winds between guides, you must remember that in the time they worked all fine rods were of bamboo, glued together in strips, and that the adhesives used then were less versatile than those of today, as well as less dependable. Those narrow trim windings were insurance against adhesive failures. During the lifetimes of many of these craftsmen, glues became dependable, and the trim strips grew more and more narrow, and finally vanished. On modern rods of fiberglass and graphite, functional wrappings are all that are really necessary.

Perhaps because of my early conditioning, I still prefer the elegance of understatement in rod windings rather than the garish kind that seem to be shouting for attention. The windings on a rod should be like the use to which a beautiful and self-assured woman puts her perfume; you don't become conscious at once of its aroma, while the gauche and uncertain woman pours on so much perfume that its overpowering fragrance knocks you down. This is a matter of personal opinion, and I grant you others may differ from mine.

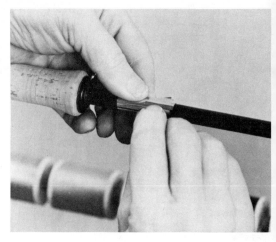

Spiral decorative windings over a contrasting color of thread, paint, or some
thin metallic material such as Mylar
are very easy to apply. When using
Mylar, cut a strip of the desired width,
allowing about a 1/16-inch overlap.
Brush color preservative on the blank
at the point where the Mylar starts,
and when the Mylar has been
smoothed on the blank, brush its surface with preservative to give some
"tooth" for the winding thread.

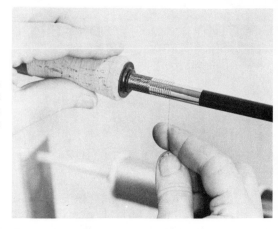

Lay on a solid wind over the end of the
Mylar, spiral the thread up the foil as
shown, and anchor the Mylar with a
second solid wrap beginning about
1/16 to 1/8 inch from its end.

Let's look at a couple of decorative trim windings. One is based on the
simple spiral already discussed. Mark the area the spiral will cover and un-
derlay it with Mylar, rod-winding tape, enamel, or nail polish in a suitable
shade. Over-wind the edges of the area covered by the contrasting material
or color. Consult the pictures for the technique. (This, by the way, is the
only place where I recommend using rod-winding tape. I experimented
with this tape quite extensively and found that it is simply not stable
enough to be used in fitting guides. When used as a decorative accent,
anchored by thread, it is quite satisfactory.)

Finally, we come to the spiral or diamond butt wind, made much easier
with Gudebrod's Butt Wind, a woven strip that requires only a pair of
threads on each side to form a pattern that looks complicated but is really
rather easy to wind if you proceed with methodical care. Once more, the
pictures illustrate the method more clearly than could several paragraphs
of text.

While still concentrating on the area around a rod's grip, we might look at the wound-on grip check, which began life as a functional winding and now has become associated with fine custom rods. It, too, is easier to apply than it looks. The secret is in fairing the tip of the cork grip to the blade of the rod. Do this with a small dab of cork adhesive, already referred to, a mixture of fine cork dust and adhesive. Sand it very carefully when dry to make a smooth joint. Coat the joint well with white shellac, and when the shellac has dried, just before beginning to wind the check, put a coat of color preservative on the area to be wound. Then wind from the blank over the tip of the cork grip and finish off with a pull-loop as you would any other winding. The hook keeper is wound on as part of the butt trim, and goes on just like a guide. If you're using one of Allan's combination hook-keeper/leader trimmers, set it fairly high above the top of the grip.

Tiptops should give you no trouble. You have the choice of winding to the bottom of the top's barrel, or tapering the barrel's rim and climbing the thread up over it as you would over a guide foot. Or, if you prefer, a method of fairing the tiptop's barrel into the blank is shown in a later chapter; this makes winding up the barrel much easier.

Diamond Butt Wind

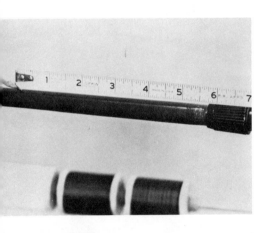

1. Begin a spiral or diamond decorative butt wind by marking off the area it will span; the most popular spacing is ½ inch. Mark both sides of the blank.

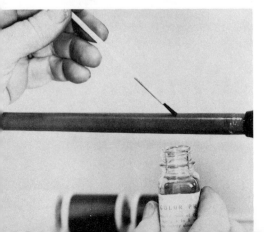

2. Brush color preservative over the area the wind will cover.

3. Use masking tape in thin strips to tie in the threads. Gudebrod's Butt Wind (TM) simplifies putting on this kind of trim. The Butt Wind is anchored at approximately the angle it will take when spiraled up the blank.

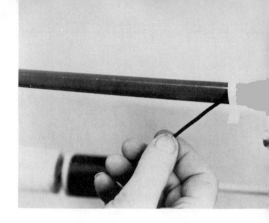

4. Carry the Butt Wind up the blank, being sure that each turn goes directly over one of the spacing marks. Spiral the Butt Wind up to the point where the marks end, then down, crossing the first spiral directly over the marks. Anchor with another strip of tape.

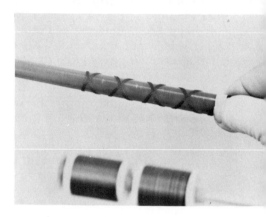

5. Anchor a trim thread of a contrasting color directly beside one side of the Butt Wind.

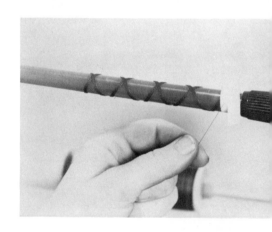

6. Carry the thread up beside the spiraled Butt Wind, then down, and anchor with tape. Use a fresh strip of tape for each anchor.

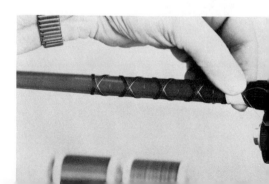

7. Repeat this with a second, and, if you wish, a third thread. You must wind all courses of trim thread on the same side of the Butt Wind before adding thread to the other side.

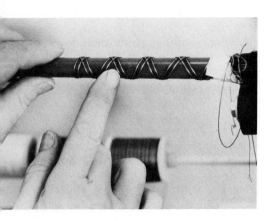

8. Repeat the winding of individual trim threads on the opposite side of the Butt Wind from the completed trim. This forms the diamond at each crossing of threads and Butt Wind. Finish with a course of the same color thread on each side.

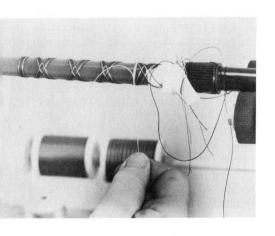

9. Make a six- or eight-turn temporary anchor wind just above the point where the bottom spiral is formed and start your permanent anchoring finish wind just below the crossing of the first spiral.

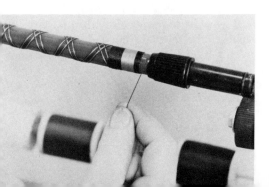

10. When the finish winding is well along, remove all masking tape and trim the Butt Wind and threads with scissors. Finish off the bottom winding in single- or multi-toned thread and pull through in the usual manner at the top of the butt ferrule.

71

VARNISH

Modern rod makers have a choice of protective finishes that go far beyond plain spar varnish. More importantly, modern blanks of graphite and fiberglass need no protective coating except at the windings; this is something that can be fully appreciated only if you've varnished bamboo rods for their entire length.

Both Gudebrod and Featherweight market very good epoxy coatings that are easy to use and generally require only a single coat to protect a rod's windings. Be sure to follow the makers' directions in detail, though. The big advantage of epoxy coatings is the short time required for their surfaces to harden; this prevents dust and airborne debris from settling on them if you take ordinary care. To keep windings from turning color, you must use a color preservative unless you've wound the rod with a thread treated to be immune to such change. The only such thread I know of is Gudebrod's NPC (No Protective Coating) thread. It does not change color when either varnish or epoxy coatings are put on it.

When using any other kind of thread, be sure to begin the coating job with a color preservative and let the thread dry thoroughly before beginning to varnish. Use a fine brush to apply the preservative; the easiest way to work is with the rod resting in a holder, so that it can be rotated with one hand while using the other to apply the coating. Use a toothpick to get into the areas around the feet of the guides, below the rings. The drying time for color preservative is usually quoted on labels as ten minutes, but to be safe, let it dry twice that long before starting to varnish.

"Varnish" is really an inaccurate word to use in describing modern coatings. Most of them are based on resin or polyurethane or epoxy, and all of them are equally easy to use and equally satisfactory in giving long service. For many years, I've used Fuller's Cleer, which is polyurethane-based. It has an unusually long storage life, doesn't film over or cake if the can is closed tightly, and is available in two finishes, satin and glossy. I've used both finishes, and like the satin better than the glossy. It dries to a moderate sheen that seems to enhance the windings it covers. This is another question of personal taste; many prefer the glossy finish.

Avoid thick coats of varnish or epoxy. They're popular as this is written, on factory rods, but some rods I've seen have such thickly varnished or epoxied windings that they seem unpleasantly lumpy.

Unless you object to getting varnish on your hands—and you're going to get some on them anyhow, no matter how carefully you work—apply the first coat of varnish with your fingertips. Work across the grain of the winding, rubbing in the varnish to fill all the tiny spaces between the threads. Your objective is to create a perfectly smooth surface on which to apply the finishing coat or coats. In most cases, if you do the job well with the first coat, a second coat applied with a brush will be all that's needed.

Let the first coat dry overnight or even longer if the humidity is high, in an atmosphere as dust-free as you can create. If you have a spare bathroom, you can make a dust-free atmosphere by closing it tightly and letting hot water run in the tub or shower until the room's full of steam. Keep the door closed while the steam carries the dust particles in the air to the floor, and then hang the rod sections up to dry.

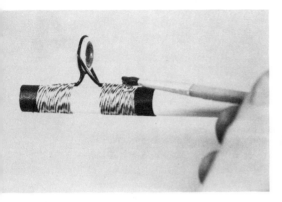

When applying color preservative, varnish, or clear epoxy protective coatings to windings, put on the first coat by holding the filled brush at a slight angle to the winding and rotating the rod in its rest. When using epoxy, follow the maker's directions. Apply the second coat by brushing up and down along the winding.

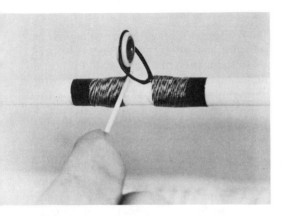

A drop on a toothpick tip reaches behind the feet of the guides, which must be filled to keep moisture from entering between foot and blank and causing the thread to discolor.

Apply the final coat with a small brush, feathering the varnish at the edges of the windings to the surface of the rod. Again, work with the rod on a rest and also use a toothpick to work the varnish behind the feet of the guides, where there's always a gap between rod and thread. Do this before applying the varnish with a brush. If your first coat has been applied carefully, you'll have no trouble getting a smooth surface. Before putting the work aside to dry, inspect each wind for bubbles, blobs, and voids. Use the point of a cocktail toothpick to puncture bubbles, and if you pick up a blob and remove it, flow a tiny bit of varnish on to replace what you've removed.

As soon as the final coat has dried, you're ready to take your new rod out and go fishing with it.

4

Cane Fishing Poles

MOST ANGLERS WHO in the 1970s are forty or more years of age very probably took their first fish with a cane pole, when they were youngsters just entering the angling world. A lot of fishermen of all ages still ply a cane pole now and then, and let's not put down this method of fishing as being primitive or unsportsmanlike. Primitive, perhaps, as the cane pole is the ancestor of the built-up fishing rod. Unsportsmanlike, not by any stretch of the imagination.

Stillfishing with a cane pole or its modern fiberglass equivalent, the long one-piece or telescoping glass pole, can be a very challenging sport indeed. No other style of angling imposes the need for such intimate knowledge of the water on those who use it, or forces the fisherman to stalk the fish he's after with such stealth and cunning. No other method of fishing, whether done from bank or boat, brings angler and fish into such close proximity. The very limitations of the cane pole, with its restricted amount of line, require an entirely different approach than does the long cast with a short rod. Perhaps these are reasons why cane-pole stillfishing will always be enjoyed.

Generally, a cane pole is rigged only one way: with a line a few feet longer than the pole tied to its tip. Given a cane pole 12 feet long, the fisherman can cover only a limited area of water, for his casting is a matter of flopping out the short line, or, as often, lowering it cautiously into a pocket a dozen feet away.

This is the pristine form of cane-pole fishing, but it can be improved. Casting distance can be increased as much as 30 to 50 percent by bringing the line to the butt of the pole and giving better control of it to the fisherman. With a reel of some sort, he can gather several feet of line into one hand and make a gentle swooping cast to get the bait into a likely pocket 20 to 30 feet away. Equipping a cane pole to do this costs very little money and takes very little time. It's just a matter of fitting the pole with a couple of guides, a tiptop, and a rudimentary reel seat. With a pole fitted in this fashion, the angler can not only present his bait further, but can fish it deeper than would be possible with a line tied directly to the pole's tip. This will add immensely to fishing pleasure and effectiveness.

Few cane-pole anglers take the trouble to fit up a pole. This might be because they consider poles expendable; while the man with a built-up rod invests a considerable sum in his tackle, the cane pole can be replaced for a couple of inflated dollars. Unless the pole is a thick-walled Calcutta, its useful life is at best two or three years. Calcutta canes are virtually impossible to find these days. They're as scarce as the Tonkin cane from which fine split bamboo rods are made, and Tonkin is as rare as virtue in a massage parlor at midnight. Almost all the cane poles sold today are of thin-walled domestic or Central American bamboo, white and fragile.

My impression, based on conversations with a number of cane-pole fishermen, is that few of them go to the effort of fitting one with guides, because the guides will cost them as much as the pole, and given the short life span of the pole they simply look on fittings as being money wasted. This isn't quite correct, though, because guides and other fittings can be transferred to the next cane pole bought, and the money invested in them will be justified by such prolonged use. That's one reason this chapter's included.

There's no reason to throw the baby out with its bathwater. When you buy a good cane pole, fit it out with a minimum number of guides, three to five depending on its length, a tiptop, and a modest reel seat. Then, prolong its life by giving it a coat of varnish. This will retard splitting and cracking of the cane's thin outer wall, which cause it to get soupy and eventually break when a good fish is being hauled in.

The fittings needed for equipping a cane pole include a few large ring guides, a tiptop with a large barrel, and, if you want to go that far, a surface-mounted reel seat. Or you can take an even simpler route in the reel-seat department by using plastic electrician's tape to hold the reel seat in place, even mounting guides with this same tape. On a couple of fitted cane poles I've seen, small hose clamps have been used in place of a reel seat.

Electrician's tape is chancy to use in winding on guides. It softens when hot and gets brittle when cold. Heavy wrapping thread is better, and 6- to 8-pound-test braided casting line is better yet. It goes on fast, is easy to handle, and only a couple of feet of this line will take care of all the windings a cane pole requires. The method used in fitting the guides is the same as that detailed in Chapter 3. Four guides will take care of a 12-foot cane pole. Space them equally from about 18 to 20 inches above the reel to within 12 inches or so of the tiptop.

A saltwater rod tiptop will probably be needed, as the tips of cane poles are much larger in diameter than those of even the heaviest freshwater rods. This doesn't mean a roller tip, of course, just a regular braced tip. Or use one of the rodstraddling tiptops in the Gudebrod line of Aetna Foulproof guides. These have feet that go on either side of the rod tip.

Surface-mounted reel seats are easy to install and require no bushings or any other kind of fitting or gluing. They're also very dependable. During the tackle-scarce days of World War II, when travel restrictions kept me from my favorite Sierra trout streams, I began fishing for striped bass in the bays around San Francisco. This was the first saltwater fishing I'd done in a number of years. I had no suitable tackle, and none was available, new or used. Calcutta cane poles were still on the market, so I fitted one with

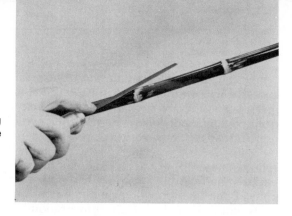

Prepare a cane pole for winding a handle on by smoothing the nodes or joints with a file.

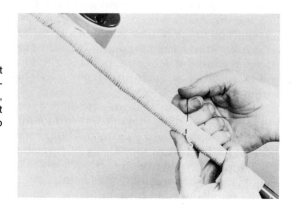

Wind on the handle or grip just as you'd wind a guide, incorporating the reel feet in this case, and fray the ends of the light cord before pulling through to avoid a bulge.

Fitting a cane pole with a grip, reel, and guides contributes to the pleasure of this style of angling.

guides and a home-made surface-mounted reel seat, put on a knuckle-buster reel, a relic that had been lurking forgotten in a corner of my tackle box, and used the outfit for several years without any problems.

Most tackle shops stock some type of surface-mounted reel seat, which can be wound on a cane pole or telescoping "whipout." Childre has a gadget called a "line tender," which isn't a reel or reel seat, but a sort of bobbin that can be used to store and adjust line length. Berkley makes an inexpensive plastic reel that's not designed for casting, but for cane poles; it costs less than $2.00. Be sure to wrap on your reel seat with casting line or winding thread; the same flaws that make electrician's tape unsuitable for winding on guides apply equally to its use in attaching reel seats.

You can, of course, wrap the reel directly on the pole as part of a cord handle. This method beats hose clamps, which have sharp, projecting corners and edges. Get about 6 feet of $^3/_{16}$- or $^1/_4$-inch cotton utility cord, file the nodes off the butt of the pole to give you a smooth working area, and wind as shown in the pictures. Be sure to fray the ends wound under and pulled under to avoid a bulge.

Telescoping poles are even easier to fit up than are those of cane. Childre has slip-on guides that fit neatly at the end of each section, so you lose nothing in portability. However, I like folding guides better, because they hold the line high off the pole. Use a guide at the end of each section, and when you get ready to go home just fold it flat to make carrying easy and snag-free.

You can wrap a telescoping pole as readily as one of cane, but you might be more comfortable with one of the preformed foam plastic grips that take the cramp out of fingers holding a small-diameter pole for a long while. Featherweight's Foamlite and Hypalon grips are available in inside

Equipping a telescoping pole with a folding guide at each joint will hold the line away from the pole; when the guide is folded, the pole is conveniently flat for carrying.

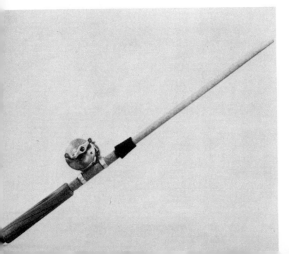

On this telescoping pole, the butt grip is a slip-on made by Gladding; the reel seat is made from sheet cork attached with Pliobond adhesive; the keeper rings were cut from aluminum conduit connectors—see text for the method of making them; and the foregrip is the shroud from a Rawhide auxiliary butt ferrule.

diameters of up to $7/8$ inch, which is bigger than any telescoping pole I've seen. They simply slide into place, and you can dribble a few drops of adhesive under them to hold them in place, though they don't really need this. Gladding has slip-on grips made of cellulite; these come with IDs of up to $9/16$ inch, and like the others just mentioned, are simply pushed into position.

For a reel seat on the telescoping pole pictured, I used cork sheeting attached with Pliobond; it took only two layers to build up a reel seat. The rings are from $1/2$-inch conduit connectors, and in a later chapter you'll find how to make them. The grips in the picture are Gladding's Gladgrips.

A cane pole or telescoping fiberglass pole can be made into an individualized job that will give you as much pride of ownership as a custom rod, with a lot less work and cost. More important, it makes your fishing days easier and more pleasant.

5

Baitcast/Spincast Rods

WHAT WE CALL a baitcast/spincast rod today is the direct descendant of the 7- to 8-foot baitcasting rod that was America's unique contribution to the angling arts. Today's rods are shorter, their actions much improved, and they're made of new materials, but the line of descent is direct and unmistakable. An angler from the 1820s would recognize such a rod at a glance.

Baitcasting rods were designed originally to flip a heavy live bait with a sidearm cast under the brush that overhung the shores of Southern bass waters. Very heavy live baits were used in the period before the early 1900s. In one of his fishing stories, written between 1906 and 1910, Zane Grey tells of using "medium sized six-inch shiners" when fishing for bass on the Delaware, so a big shiner would have been in the 8- to 10-inch range. Other popular baits of the era were live frogs and crayfish. Early baitcasting rods were equipped with reels far less responsive than those of today, and lines were heavy braided affairs of linen or untreated silk that had as much water-repelling capacity as a sponge. Of necessity, the early baitcasting rods were 7 to 8 feet long, rarely 6 feet or shorter, with very stiff action.

Lures were heavy, too, big spinners and spoons, until the first cedar "plugs" appeared in the 1880s. With the advent of the light wooden—and, later, plastic—lures, with improved lines and reels, baitcasting rods grew lighter and shorter. The closed-face spincast reel proved especially adaptable to existing baitcasting rods, and so the present baitcast/spincast rods evolved, 5 to 6 feet long, with tips versatile enough to flip out lures weighing as little as $1/_8$ ounce. Today, your choice of a blank on which to make a baitcast/spincast rod is governed by several factors: where you fish, the weight-range of lures you customarily use, and the kind of water you visit most often.

There are four basic actions built into modern baitcast/spincast rod blanks. "Light-tip" or "fast-tip" blanks—these terms are used somewhat interchangeably by manufacturers and describe the same type of blank—

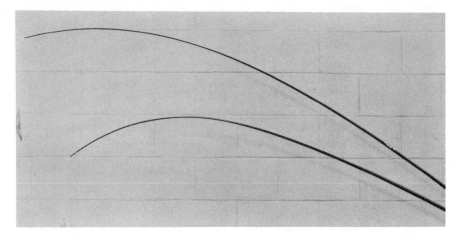

In a parabolic action or straight-taper baitcast/spincast rod (top) the action is well distributed into the butt area. The blank below it has fast-tip action, concentrated in its upper third. Both blanks are being held at the same angle and their tips carry the same amount of weight.

have thin walls and large butts that taper to a delicate tip that is designed to cast light lures a comparatively short distance. Parabolic blanks have a uniform taper that distributes the action or flexing along the entire length of the rod so that under strain it takes the shape of a parabola; these are perhaps best suited for general-purpose use. Progressive tapers marry the delicate tip of the fast-action blank to the even taper of the parabolic blank for middle- to long-distance light lure casts. Straight-taper blanks are the *machos* of the rod world; they are usually given a manufacturer's description implying great strength, which indeed they have; they handle a wide range of lure weights at middle distances.

Not all manufacturers offer blanks in each of these groups, so you'll have to acquaint yourself with the lines offered by all the leading makers to be sure of getting the kind of action best suited to your most frequent fishing requirements. If you usually fish light, virtually weightless lures such as plastic worms in quiet, brush-free waters, a fast or light tip blank might suit you best. If you go into snag-filled lakes seeking lunker bass that must be snaked up quickly to avoid tangles on underwater snags, the straight-taper blank is probably what you're looking for. If you use a variety of lures in many different places, the two middle-range, all-purpose blanks will meet your requirements. But you should try to test each type before making up your mind what you want.

On all baitcast/spincast rods you can switch from a revolving spool to a closed-face fixed spool reel without experiencing problems in casting. This is not due to the design of the rods, but to the line-feed characteristics of the reels; if you tried to use an open-face spinning reel on a rod fitted with baitcast/spincast guides, your casting would suffer. A baitcasting reel feeds line to the butt guide of a rod along a horizontal path of no more than 2 or 3 inches, and a closed-face spincast reel has virtually a straight-line feed

BUTT GUIDE

Location of the butt guide on a baitcast/spincast rod should take into consideration the width of the spool on your baitcasting reel. The guide should be
placed far enough from the reel seat so that the line will just touch the sides
of the butt guide when at either side of the reel spool. See text for details.

path. Open-face spinning reels feed line in a funnel-shaped spiral that
must be contained or controlled by an oversized butt guide. If you switch
between these two types of reels, then the versatile baitcast/spincast rod is
for you.

Blanks of this type are generally fitted with a butt ferrule that fits either a
collet or an oversized female ferrule at the top of the grip. Grips are thus
interchangeable; you can, if you wish, use a pistol-handle, straight-handle,
or offset handle—whichever type suits you best. You can also use a straight,
chuck-headed grip of the type used on spinning rods, if you wish.

Baitcast/spincast rods are the easiest of all types to make. You need the
blank that has the action you wish, a handle, a set of guides, and winding
thread and protective coating. In choosing guides, let the reel you intend to
use dictate the butt guide's size. If you use a spincast or narrow-spool baitcasting reel, your butt guide can be as small as 10mm to 12mm; if you use a
wide-spool baitcasting reel, go up to a 14mm or 15mm butt guide, stepping
down toward the tip to one or more 5mm guides. It will be greatly to your
advantage to get ceramic or aluminum oxide insert guides; they reduce line
friction and are very resistant to scoring. The short blanks, $4^{1}/_{2}$ to 6 feet,
used in making baitcast/spincast rods are very rarely center-ferruled.

Begin by making the all-important test that will locate the blank's spine;
this is detailed in Chapter 3. After you've located the spine side of the blank
and marked it so that you can locate it at butt and tip when you next need
to refer to it, your next step is to set the butt ferrule.

If the blank you're working on is graphite and the butt ferrule wasn't installed at the factory, you should plug the butt before setting the ferrule.
The plug in a graphite blank should extend above the top of the ferrule by
about 2 to 3 inches. Use an easily worked wood such as basswood or ash and
rough-taper the plug with a file, then sand it to match the inner wall of the
blank. Be sure to round the top end of the plug so that it won't press
against the wall. Set the plug with Pliobond or epoxy.

Butt ferrules are sized to fit any diameter blank from $^{20}/_{64}$ to $^{40}/_{64}$ inch;
their inside diameters step up through this entire range in 64ths. In the
decimal fractions used by most blank manufacturers when giving butt diameter dimensions, these ferrules range from .312 to .625 of an inch. You
should have no problem getting an exact fit for your blank. The chucks on
virtually all preformed baitcast/spincast rod grips accept a ferrule with a
bottom spindle diameter of $^{3}/_{8}$ inch, and older grips that accept different
diameter spindles can be used with one of the converter ferrules sold by
both Featherweight and Childre-Fuji.

Fitting The Butt Ferrule

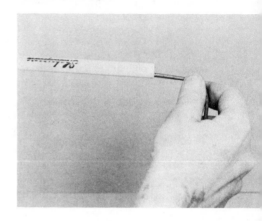

1. When fitting the plug in the butt of a baitcast/spincast blank, apply adhesive to both the plug and the inner wall of the blank. Use a length of stout wire to reach inside the blank.

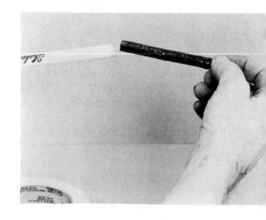

2. Slide the adhesive-coated plug into the butt.

3. Close the butt of the blank with masking tape and sit the blank as nearly vertical as possible until the adhesive sets up.

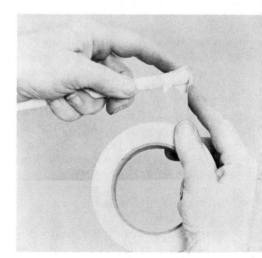

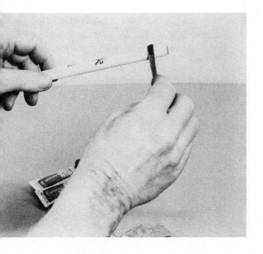

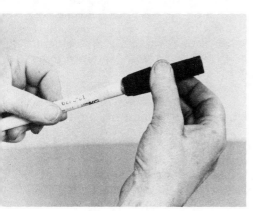

4. Sand the butt to fit snugly into the type of butt ferrule it will require, then coat the butt with adhesive.

5. Slide the ferrule into place and let the adhesive begin to set before wiping off the excess. This will give you a smooth joint for the butt trim.

GUIDE SPACING

You're now ready to go on to the job that will determine whether your new rod will be a joy to use or will have an erratic and unsatisfactory action in casting. This is the spacing of the guides. Testing is the only way of definitely ascertaining whether this spacing is satisfactory. While blanks are manufactured to very precise standards, each blank is individual in its action. The difference may be almost microscopically small, but it's there. All that can be done here is to give you a table of approximate spacings for blanks of different lengths and actions with a caution that the approximations might not be ideal for all blanks.

There are a lot of guide-spacing charts floating around, and I dug up all of them that I could find to check their suggestions. I also measured spacings on my own baitcast/spincast rods and on a dozen or so factory rods from different manufacturers. The diversity was tremendous. No two charts agreed, none of my own rods had precisely the same spacings, and neither did the factory rods. The differences ranged from 7 inches in the spacing of butt guides (measured from the reel spool) to $2^1/_2$ inches in that of top guides measured from the rod tip. All the rods measured were grouped by length and action.

Few of the charts offered anything other than exact spacings, which I considered somewhat dangerous, as most of them were designed to be used with one specific blank from one specific manufacturer. It occurred to me that someone using them hastily or without realizing their specific nature might transfer the exact spacings they gave to a blank for which the spacings weren't intended. And I found it somewhat difficult to reconcile the wide variation, especially in butt-guide spacings, for I consider the relationship of this guide to the reel spool to be an important factor in overall rod performance.

Even when a baitcast/spincast rod is fitted with the best guides—those having aluminum oxide or ceramic inserts that are virtually friction-free—the reel to butt-guide distance is important. The function of this guide is to gather the line as it feeds from one side of the spool to the other and send it in a straight path to the next guide, as well as to hold the line above the rod's surface so that it will not cling when wet. Eventually, I resolved the problems by testing a number of rods with different reels and lure weights. The rods tested ranged all the way from a $^3/_8$-ounce tournament rod to heavy-duty jobs designed to horse a big bass out of a tangle of lily pads in the shortest possible time.

What I finally arrived at was a chart that gives you a range of spacings as suggestions from which you can work out the ideal guide spacing for the blanks on which you're working. The spacings aren't intended to be binding or definitive, and the ultimate job of tuning up your rod is up to you. The chart also includes suggestions as to the butt-guide sizes, because in my opinion the butt guides on many baitcast/spincast rods are undersized. Given the butt-guide size, it's a fairly simple matter to graduate the remaining guides a step or two down with each succeeding guide up to the tip. If you start with a butt guide in the 14mm–16mm range you can safely step down to 10mm–12mm, then to a couple of 8mm, and wind up with a 6mm–7mm guide below the tiptop. This means five guides on a 5- or $5^1/_2$-foot rod, and on 6-foot blanks you might want to add one more guide. This will depend on the blank's weight and action, and you're the only one who can decide whether or not that extra guide is needed after you've tested the blank's response to flexing with the guides in place temporarily.

Remember that guide spacing represents a series of compromises. Too many will increase line friction and slow down your casts or cause you to sacrifice distance. Too few will create line slap, or allow the line to touch the rod's surface, and may also overstress the blank by failing to distribute the stress over a large enough area. However, given the friction-free slickness of modern guides, if you must err, let it be in the direction of one guide too many rather than one too few.

Here's the chart that will give you the starting point needed to establish guide size and spacing on baitcast/spincast rods:

GUIDE SPACING FOR BAITCAST/SPINCAST RODS

BLANK ACTION		FAST TIP		
LENGTH	5'	5¹/₂'	6'	6¹/₂'
GUIDES	4"–6"	4"–6"	4"–6"	4"–6"
SPACED	10"–12"	10"–12"	10"–12"	10"–12"
FROM TIP	17"–19"	18¹/₂"–20¹/₂"	17¹/₂"–19¹/₂"	18"–20"
	25"–27"	27"–29"	25¹/₂"–27¹/₂"	27¹/₂"–29¹/₂"
	32"–34"	38"–40"	33¹/₂"–35¹/₂"	38¹/₂"–40¹/₂"
			44"–46"	50"–52"
BUTT GUIDE	12–14mm	12–14mm	12–14mm	12–14mm

BLANK ACTION		PARABOLIC/PROGRESSIVE TAPER		
LENGTH	5'	5¹/₂'	6'	6¹/₂'
GUIDES	4"–6"	4"–6"	4"–6"	4"–6"
SPACED	10"–12"	10¹/₂"–12¹/₂"	10¹/₂"–12¹/₂"	10¹/₂"–12¹/₂"
FROM TIP	16¹/₂"–18¹/₂"	19"–21"	17¹/₂"–19¹/₂"	18¹/₂"–20¹/₂"
	24"–26"	28"–30"	25¹/₂"–27¹/₂"	28"–30"
	33"–35"	38"–40"	33¹/₂"–35¹/₂"	37¹/₂"–39¹/₂"
			43"–45"	49¹/₂"–51¹/₂"
BUTT GUIDE	14–16mm	14–16mm	14–16mm	14–16mm

BLANK ACTION		STRAIGHT TAPER		
LENGTH	5'	5¹/₂'	6'	6¹/₂'
GUIDES	4"–6"	4"–6"	4"–6"	4"–6"
SPACED	9¹/₂"–11¹/₂"	10"–12"	10"–12"	10¹/₂"–12¹/₂"
FROM TIP	17¹/₂"–19¹/₂"	18¹/₂"–20¹/₂"	18"–20"	18¹/₂"–20¹/₂"
	26"–28"	27¹/₂"–29¹/₂"	27"–29"	28¹/₂"–30¹/₂"
	34¹/₂"–36¹/₂"	38¹/₂"–40¹/₂"	35¹/₂"–37¹/₂"	38¹/₂"–40¹/₂"
			44¹/₂"–46¹/₂"	46¹/₂"–48¹/₂"
BUTT GUIDE	14–16mm	14–16mm	14–16mm	14–16mm

You'll notice several things about the foregoing chart. The first feature that jumps out at you is the uniform spacing between the top guide and the tiptop. The reason for this is pretty obvious. Not only is the tip the most delicate area of any rod, insofar as taking the strain of playing a fish is concerned, but those two top guides determine the sensitivity or "feel" that the finished rod will have. Putting them too close together diminishes the sensitivity, while putting them too far apart to improve the feel may very well subject the rod to too much stress when you're handling a fish.

You'll also notice that the suggested spacings leave a pretty uniform 24- to 26-inch distance between the reel spool and the butt guide. The measurements were all taken with the rods fitted with a standard chuck-and-collet detachable grip, so you might want to shift them if you fit your rod with a straight grip that lacks the extra 2 to 3 inches taken up by the chuck. The accompanying picture shows why the butt-guide spacings are uniform, and also shows why a butt guide larger than those usually set on rods of this type is a pretty solid idea. Guide measurements, by the way, are

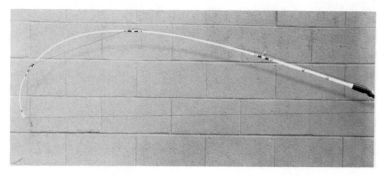

This bargain-basement baitcast/spincast rod is a good example of bad guide placement. Notice how the line crosses the blade of the rod and rubs it when under a stress equal to that of handling a good fish.

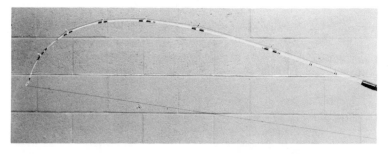

Adding more guides is the solution to this problem. In the case of the rod pictured, three guides were added, and all except the butt guide were relocated. Now, the line is clear of the blade when the rod is under stress.

quickly being standardized by tackle manufacturers in millimeters, and the outside diameter of the ring rather than the inside diameter is coming into more and more common use. Measurements in the chart are to the ring of the guide, not its foot.

Now, don't take the chart as gospel. The measurements give you a lot of leeway, though you should find the centers fairly close; that is, in a 2-inch span, the ring of the guide ought to be very nearly above the 5-inch line for the top guide and the corresponding centerline of all the other spans.

Test the spacing of your blank by fitting the guides with masking tape before winding them on. Fit a tiptop with masking tape, being sure its eye is in line with the spine. Here again we enter an area of opinion. As noted earlier, I like to set guides of baitcast/spincast and heavy saltwater rods on the spine, and those of fly and spinning rods opposite the spine. Perhaps it's my imagination, but I think these settings bring out the best in rods of each type, both in casting and in handling a hooked fish. I have absolutely no scientific data to support my belief, but have never seen any such data refuting it. Mark it down as a personal foible and set the guides as you choose yourself, on the spine or 180° around the blank from it.

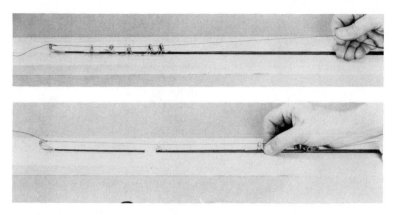

How to position and align guides in two easy steps. In the top picture, the rod
has been taped with the tiptop upright on a flat surface; the top has already
been fixed permanently so that its ring is in line with the spine. Tie a length of
cord to the top's ring at the center of its upward arc and string the guides on
it in sequence. Align the other end of the cord on the spine mark at the
blank's butt and hold in place with masking tape. In the second picture, the
guides are being placed and aligned at the same time. As long as the cord
passes through the center of a guide, that guide is in line with all the others.
Hold the guides in position temporarily with strips of masking tape during
testing and, later, winding. This method works on any kind of rod.

To get back to the business at hand, line up the tiptop's ring with the
spine mark; tie a string to it so that the string is at the top center of the ring,
and slide the guides on the string in the sequence in which they will be fitted. Pull the other end of the string straight but not taut and align it with
the spine reference mark at the butt of the blank. Hold it with masking tape
while you measure the guide spacings, and put the guides in place with
strips of tape. This is the easiest way to assure a perfectly straight line of
guides.

TESTING

The next step is to mount a reel and put on a practice plug, go outdoors
and make some experimental casts. If you find the guide spacing creates
line drag or slap, or if the tip response doesn't feel right, shift the guides up
or down the blade until you're satisfied. Even precision-made blanks will
vary a bit, just as do the casting styles of anglers. The only rule that really
works in guide spacing is rule of thumb, and all the charts can do is give
you a starting point.

You might find it necessary to add or remove a guide. If line slap is the
trouble, it's a pretty good indication that your blank is one guide short. If
tip vibration bothers you—though this is rare in modern, computer-
designed blanks—try weighting the tip with a tiny bit of lead. The easiest
kind to use is that which you can pull from the core of a lead-weighted
trolling line. You need only a scrap. Just slip the core out of its braided covering and tap it into a thin strip. This lead is more ductile than any small-

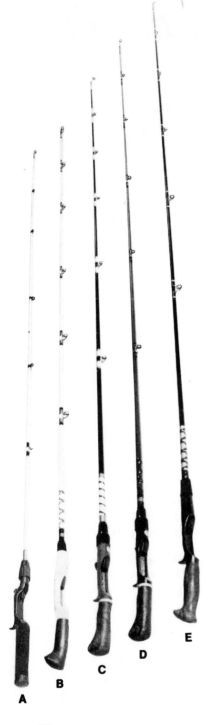

Baitcast/Spincast Rods

A **Ultra-light:** Plas/Steel (solid fiberglass); color, white
Length: 5′, 1-piece
Weight: Blank, 1⅝ ounce; fitted, 3 oz (not including handle)
Handle: Featherweight 6AH30
Guides: Butt, Allan ceramic; running, Fuji Speed Slip-On
Winding: Butt guide, Gudebrod black #001, side A

B **Light:** Shakespeare #120239 blank; color, white
Length: 5′ 6″, 1-piece
Weight: Blank, 1⅞ oz; fitted, 3⅛ oz (not including handle)
Handle: Fuji OBBC
Guides: Fuji ceramic BSHG series
Winding: Gudebrod size A; primary black/white #8002; trim, black #001

C **Medium-light:** Childre blank #6158B; color, black
Length: 5′ 6″, 1-piece
Weight: Blank, 1⅞ oz; fitted, 2⅝ oz (not including handle)
Handle: Fuji OBBC
Guides: Allan CER ceramic series
Winding: Gudebrod size D; primary white #002; trim, black #001

D **Medium:** Sabre blank #196SL; color, amber
Length: 5′ 6″, 1-piece
Weight: Blank, 2¹/₁₆ oz; fitted, 3⅞ oz (not including handle)
Handle: Fuji OCBC
Guides: Varmac ceramic AT series
Winding: Gudebrod size D; space dye orange/black #0122

E **Heavy:** Rawhide blank #6010F; color, maroon
Length: 6′, 1-piece
Weight: Blank, 3¼ oz; fitted, 4⅝ oz (not including handle)
Handle: Featherweight RR5K
Guides: Varmac ceramic AT series
Winding: Gudebrod size D; primary blue #230; trim maroon #337

diameter lead wire you can buy. Wrap a few turns of the strip around the tip of the blank, replace the tiptop with one $1/_{64}$th larger, and test the blank again. You might have to add or remove weight; this can be determined only by actual tests.

In some cases, you might find it necessary to go to an entirely different kind of guide. This seldom happens when you're using a medium to heavyweight blank, but a complete change may be needed if the blank is a very light one. In order of weight, ceramic insert guides are heavies, Carboloy or tungsten carbide middleweights, stainless steel lightweights. Gudebrod's Aetna Foulproof guides are the lightest of all and flex with the rod. They might be your answer to a stubborn problem.

After you've made any adjustments indicated by your casting tests, using the reels you normally fish with, make one final test. Take off the practice plug you've been using and put a weight of about 2 pounds on the line. Lift the rod slowly by the grip until it's taking the strain of the weight. Check the line path to be sure the guides are spaced closely enough to hold the line away from the rod. The line should not touch the rod at any point in its arc. If it does, put in an additional guide and space the entire set of guides more closely.

This testing will take a bit of time, but it'll be the best time you can invest. It's a bonus you get only when you make your own rod. Manufacturers turning out thousands of rods a month on their production lines can't afford to invest this amount of time testing each individual rod blank; they must install guides on the basis of averages. If they took the time you put into your rod, their rods would be priced out of the market by high labor costs. In justice, manufacturers do test prototype blanks very carefully and also make periodic cross-checks of rods pulled at random off their production lines, but the razor-edge performance that you will get by putting a blank through the series of tests just described will result in a rod that will give you maximum performance, because it's tailored to your own individual style of casting.

You're just about home free, now. All that's left to do is to set your tiptop permanently and wind on the guides. Take one final precaution. Be sure the tiptop is in alignment with the spine, and after it's set with adhesive, get out that piece of string and thread it through the guides again to be sure they, too, are in perfect alignment. Then, follow the directions in Chapter 3 to set the guides, add a bit of varnish to the windings, and as soon as the varnish is dry, head for your favorite fishing spot.

6

Spinning Rods

ALTHOUGH VIRTUALLY UNKNOWN in the United States until the late 1940s, spinning rods very quickly began moving up on the popularity scale. There are no statistics to support this, but it's probable that they have nosed bait-cast/spincast rods out of the first place position; if they haven't, it's now a neck-and-neck race. These rods were created in England to be used with the open-faced fixed-spool reel invented by Holden Illingworth in the late 1880s, and their use spread quickly to Europe. Since they were originally intended to be used with extremely fine lines, spinning was called "threadline fishing" until heavy-duty reels brought the rods into popularity among saltwater anglers.

Fishermen who favor spinning tackle have learned that in today's specialized world, one spinning rod isn't enough to cope with all fishing situations. The variety of spinning rod blanks has multiplied rapidly. You now have a choice of extremely delicate blanks of 5, $5\frac{1}{2}$, and 6 feet that really do use lines finer than sewing thread, and the range extends to husky surf and saltwater blanks 10 to 12 feet long, capable of casting a half-pound of weight and bait far out into the surf, and sturdy enough to handle almost any of the big denizens of the ocean.

Spinning rod blanks offer you three kinds of action: fast tip, parabolic, and progressive or step-down taper. Fast-tip blanks are usually the lightest in weight. Their action is concentrated in the upper third of the blank's length, which makes them very quick in casting and gives them a sensitive feel. Casting with blanks of this type requires more practice to obtain consistent accuracy but demands less effort once you've gotten the feel of the rod.

Between the fast-tip blank and the modified taper blank are the parabolics, which are also described in catalogs as "straight-taper," "medium," and "slow or "soft" action types. In these blanks the action is distributed along the entire length of the blade. Parabolics will handle a wide range of lure weights, take little practice to master and, because their power is distributed evenly, will cope with a very wide variety of fishing situations.

90

Progressive or step-down taper blanks have sensitive tips, powerful butt sections, and a central power zone that provides most of the action. Those who favor this type of blank say that the greatest amount of flexing power is concentrated in the area of the blank that carries the greatest strain. The tips of these blanks are satisfactorily sensitive, and they are versatile enough to handle both light and heavy lures.

In classifying spinning rod weights it now seems to make more sense to do so by the maximum monofil test they will handle satisfactorily rather than by the blank's weight. Graphite has changed early concepts of strength-to-weight ratios. Thus, we might say that an ultralight spinning rod blank is best suited to monofil no heavier than 4-pound test; a light one will handle monofil in the 6- to 8-pound range best; a medium blank performs most efficiently with 10- or 12-pound test mono; a heavy blank goes into the 14- to 16- or 18-pound range; and an ultraheavy blank takes care of monofil up to 24-pound test. Of course, the ranges are somewhat elastic. Almost any spinning rod blank will handle line of tests lighter than its maximum rating, but for peak efficiency, it should be used with line inside its rating.

These limits in general correspond to the limitations of spinning reels. Most of these reels have a range of three weights of monofil that they will handle without difficulty—in other words a much narrower adaptability than any other type. A mid-range spinning reel is typically designed and its gears and other components engineered to handle at best three weights of monofil. These might be 4-6-8-pound test, or 8-10-12-pound, or any other similar sequence. Any fisherman who consistently overloads an open-face spinning reel with line heavier than that for which it was designed is asking for real trouble.

Because open-face spinning reels release line in the general shape of a moving funnel or spiral, the rods on which they're used must be fitted with guides sized to control the line. The butt guide on a spinning rod has one primary function: to collect the spiraling monofil as it comes off the reel and straighten it with a minimum of drag into a straight line that will flow smoothly through the smaller guides toward the tip. Because 20-pound test monofil is much stiffer than 8- or 10-pound test, the butt guide on a rod designed to be fished with heavy lines must be larger than on those with which lower test monofil will be used.

An almost universal feature of the first spinning rods was a long grip with a pair of keeper rings that allowed the angler to shift his reel up and down on the grip to get better balance when casting—in effect, a movable reel seat. Though early spinning reels varied much more in weight than today's do, this feature is still important on light and ultralight spinning rods. Although there are small, lightweight reels available for these delicate rods, they will vary between makes by several ounces of weight.

Fixed reel seats are now universal on medium and heavy-duty spinning rods; these are generally set between a short foregrip and a long butt grip. From the standpoint of the rod maker, this means that fitting a fixed reel-seat grip involves three separate operations in a fixed sequence: first, the butt grip, then the reel seat, and finally, the foregrip. If a winding check is used, it should be put on at this time, and so should the butt cap, hosel, or cork button that finishes off the butt grip. The picture sequence gives details of these steps, and another picture shows the more common types of today's spinning rods grips and reel seats, on spinning rods of different weights and lengths.

FERRULES

After you've chosen the blank for your new spinning rod and located its spine by the methods detailed in Chapter 3, your first job is setting a ferrule—or ferrules, if the rod is to be made up into a trail or travel rod. The method for ferrule setting is also described and pictured in Chapter 3, but first let's explore the options you have in selecting the spot at which a single ferrule can be set to improve a spinning rod's performance.

To a limited but important extent, you may be able to speed up the action of a straight-taper blank by setting the ferrule a bit above the center. You can usually improve the feel of a step-down taper blank by setting the ferrule a little below the center. Remember that wherever you set your ferrule, you're going to create a flat spot in the blank, and the location of this spot will change the performance of the finished rod in casting as well as in sensitivity. You'll have to do a bit of testing to determine where the ferrule can be placed most advantageously, if you decide to set it off-center.

Holding the blank in your hand and wiggling it sidewise or up and down won't tell you a great deal. Very few people, unless they've built a lot of rods, have the experience required to translate the feels of a raw blank into its feel when it's been fitted. The action of an unfitted blank is very different from that of the finished rod made from it.

When you're searching for the spine of a blank by the second of the three methods given in Chapter 3—flexing the blank's tip while resting its butt on the floor—you'll also get a pretty shrewd idea as to where the blank's power axis is located. In a fast-tip blank, it will be in the upper third of the rod; in a parabolic blank, at or a bit below the center; in a step-down taper blank, a bit above the center, or perhaps at the center-point. Of the three, the step-down or progressive action tapered blank will show the least effect of off-center ferruling.

However, as noted, you can extend the tip of a fast-tip blank by dropping the ferrule below the center-point and, conversely, speed up the tip of a straight-taper blank by ferruling above the center. How far above or below? A good question, one that only you can answer, as each blank is an individual that has its own character. The only rule of thumb I can offer is that the ferrule should not go more than 2 or 3 inches or less than 1 to $1\frac{1}{2}$ inches above or below. You can get a rough idea by grasping the blank with one hand while flexing it with the butt on the floor with the other. It's really a matter of feel, and that's just about impossible to describe, since no two sets of hands feel in exactly the same way.

A word of caution here. If you're working with a graphite blank, be very, very careful in your flexing. Remember the explanation in Chapter 1 of the difference between the modulus of graphite and fiberglass. Don't overstress a graphite blank in your test procedures, since you might find yourself setting a ferrule where you don't really want one. These blanks respond well to the temporary flexing they undergo when you're handling a fish, but have been known to break under a static stress such as the test imposes.

You can also alter the action of a blank in other ways. One is by weighting the tip, as described in Chapter 5. This procedure can be used on spinning rods successfully. Or you can trim off an inch or two from the blank's tip or butt. Shortening the tip will slow down the casting speed at the expense of some sensitivity. Here again, we're faced with compromising. Shortening the butt will soften the blank's action and in effect increase the tip's sensitivity without having too much effect on its casting speed.

Think twice before you start trimming. Manufacturers engineer the blanks they make by computerizing formulas involving wall thickness and density, length and taper, and the modern blank you get from a reputable manufacturer will very rarely be off-standard. If you're dissatisfied and return the blank in its original condition, most firms will replace it cheerfully. They're as interested in their rare failures as they are in their successes, for analyzing the failures provides data that will keep them from recurring.

If you feel you want to trim a blank, cut no more than $^3/_4$ inch at a time and test between each cut. Three inches is the most I'd recommend if you're shortening the tip, and this much only on a blank longer than $6^1/_2$ feet. You can shorten the butt by as much as 6 inches, but trimming in this area has much less effect than does reducing the blank's tip. I always hesitate to cut a blank shorter, but there are two or three sides to every story, and I'll admit that on some occasions a little judicious trimming is called for.

GRIPS

Once you've made the test for action and fitted the ferrules—remembering to mark them so that the blank can be jointed with the spine in its proper plane—it's time to put on the grip. Here, too, you have a number of options from which to choose.

Most medium-duty spinning rods will have a butt grip of 7 to 9 inches, and a foregrip 3 to 4 inches long. Both may be longer in heavy-duty rods. The reel seat, of course, is between the two sections of the grip. Light and ultralight rods benefit from the lighter weight and often the greater flexibility of design that is afforded by a reel seat integral with the grip. A shroud, sometimes called a skeleton or cutaway reel seat, can be slipped on the grip, or a pair of simple retaining rings can be put on. Either will save a bit of weight in a very light rod.

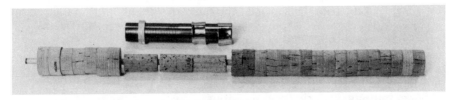

Components for a spinning-rod grip: rings for foregrip, reel-seat bushings, more rings for the butt grip. When assembled, the reel seat at rear will go over the bushings and be glued in place.

TEMPLATE PATTERNS FOR SPINNING-ROD GRIPS

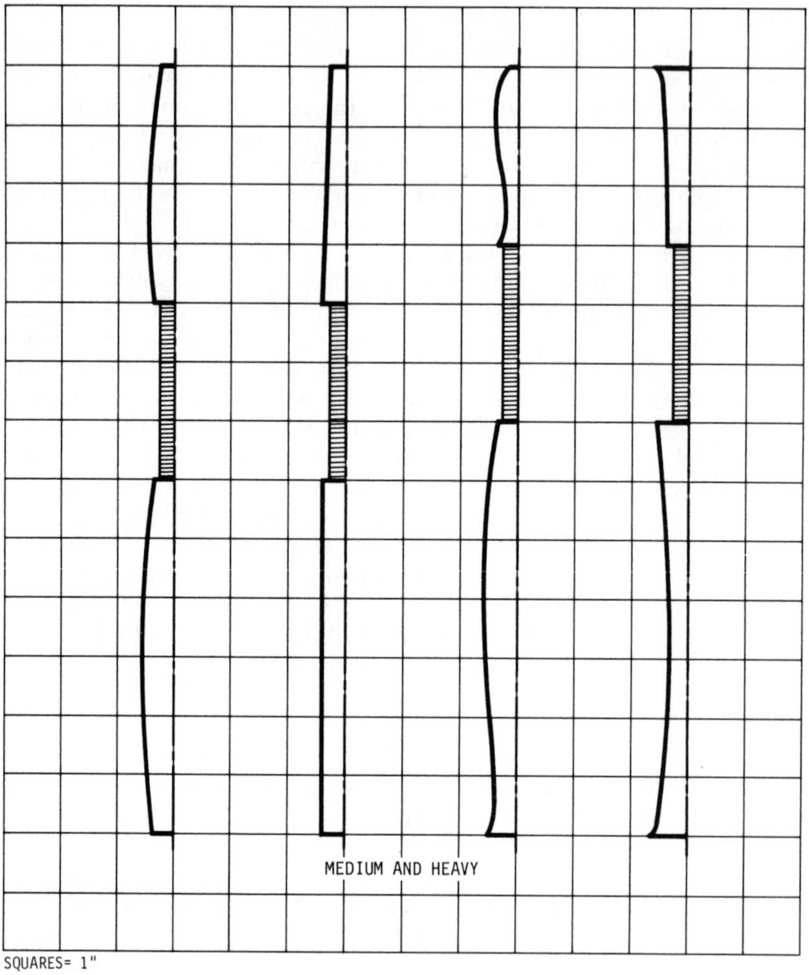

MEDIUM AND HEAVY

SQUARES= 1"

Often, if the rod is not only ultralight but short as well, it can simply be fitted with a conventional ferrule that mates with a female joint inset at the top of a separate grip. This grip can be built up separately from the rod on a piece of dowel or, for even greater lightness, on a piece cut from a discarded or broken fiberglass rod butt. Use of a separate grip makes a 5 -to 6-foot spinning rod easy to carry if the blade is center-ferruled; it becomes a travel or pack rod. Even a one-piece rod in the 5-or $5^{1}/_{2}$-foot range is not burdensome to carry if the grip is separate.

Short spinning rods, in the 6-to-7-foot range, are sometimes fitted with a butt ferrule that fits the chuck of a factory-made grip of the type used on

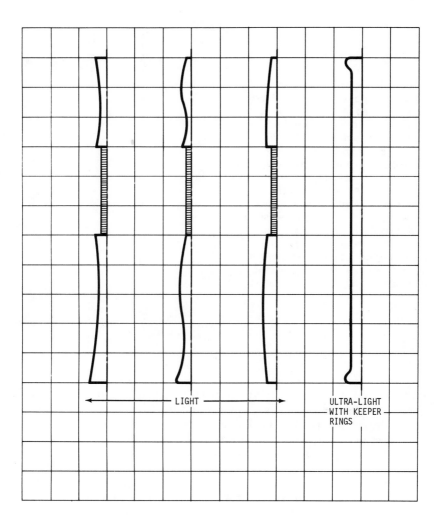

baitcast/spincast rods, except that for use on a spinning rod these grips should be longer than baitcast/spincast grips. They're available in lengths of up to 14 inches in straight, conventional spinning grip configuration or with offset reel seats. Blades fitted with a butt ferrule have a very wide choice of preformed grips with both conventional and skeleton reel seats. Again, a rod of this type can quickly be adapted to several styles of fishing just by switching its grip.

Making and forming a spinning rod grip of the style used on medium- and heavy-duty rods were covered thoroughly in Chapter 3, and here template/patterns are included to aid you in forming several different con-

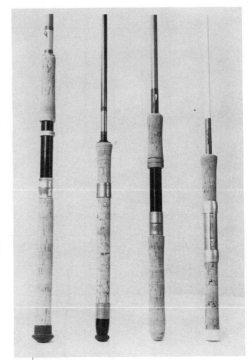

Typical spinning-rod grips. From left: heavy-duty grip on a 9-foot Sabre blank, intended for heavy-water fishing for coho, steelhead, even for light offshore use; straight grip with retainer rings on an 8½-foot Lamiglas graphite blank, used to save weight; grip on a 7½-foot Lamiglas fiberglass blank, with an Allan hood keeper that incorporates a leader clipper; straight grip with shroud or skeleton reel seat on a light Shakespeare blank, again used to save weight. The second and fourth grips have the added feature of offering a choice of reel locations anywhere along the grip.

tours. To make a working template from the pattern you choose, mark a piece of cardboard with 1-inch squares and transfer the curves of the pattern to the cardboard. Then cut along the curved lines to form the desired contour. Check with the template by stopping from time to time while forming the grip and rotating the grip against the cut-out profile.

If you're forming the grip of a spinning rod on the blank, the reel-seat bushings and reel seat must be set when you glue the cork rings to the blank. Then, protect the reel seat with several wrappings of masking tape while you file and sand the grip contours. If you're using the technique of forming the grip on threaded rod in a drill, you can form both butt grip and foregrip in the same operation, but don't glue the rings where one ends and the other starts. If you form the grip off the blank, remember that the reel-seat bushings and the reel seat must be set before the foregrip is reamed and glued. And be very sure the fixed hood on the reel seat is in line with the spine of the blank when you set it. If the guides and tiptop aren't centered on this hood you'll have to set them on a weak side of the blank, which usually makes the finished rod cast miserably.

If you're making a grip that is to be used with either a shroud reel seat or retaining rings, remember that the outside diameter of the finished grip must be the same diameter—slightly under 1 inch—along the entire length of the grip, and the side of the grip, along the spinal plane, must be filed or sanded flat so the retaining rings can be pushed firmly over the reel's feet. There are three sizes of rings available, with inside diameters of .950, 1.00,

Fitting a Spinning-Rod Grip

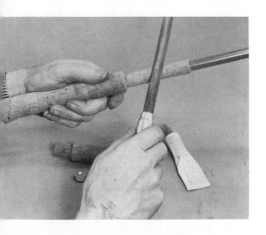

1. This spinning-rod butt grip and its still unfinished cork button butt piece has already been glued to the rod. The reel-seat bushings are being filed to the proper outside diameter to take the reel seat.

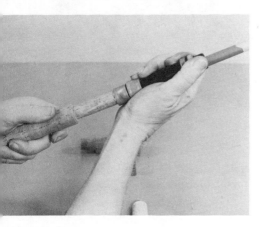

2. Adhesive has been applied to the inside of the reel seat and the outside of the bushings. When the reel seat has been pushed into firm contact with the butt grip, excess adhesive should be wiped off.

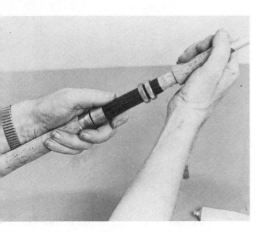

3. Adhesive has now been coated over the bushings integral with the foregrip and on the foregrip's bore, as well as on the area of the blank the foregrip will cover. The foregrip is pushed into place and excess adhesive removed.

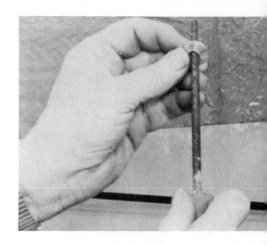

4. A grip check (also called a winding check) has been reamed to the exact inside diameter needed to fit closely on the blank above the foregrip.

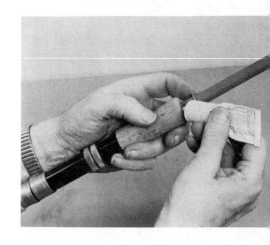

5. Adhesive is applied to the top of the foregrip. . .

6. . . .and, the winding check is pulled into position and held tightly for a few minutes until the adhesive begins to set up. Remember, these steps must be completed *before* the guides are fitted to the blank.

and 1.05 inches, really a negligible difference. Many fishermen have small hands, and I happen to be among them. You can make your own rings if you want some of a smaller diameter.

Craft aluminum tubing, easy to work, is available in tubing with outside diameters of $3/4$ and $7/8$ inch, but you can buy this material only in 6-foot lengths, and it seems wasteful to buy 72 inches of tubing to get a pair of rings $1/2$ to $3/4$ inch wide. Alternatives are thin-wall aluminum electrical conduit with a $3/4$-inch OD, or, even better, the connectors used in joining this conduit. The pictures show how to use these connectors.

To ensure that you don't take off too much material during the final sanding of a straight grip such as these ring and shroud reel seats require, make a simple measuring gauge by cutting a slot of the required width, $3/4$ to 1 inch, in a piece of cardboard or plywood and run it along the grip from time to time. Such a gauge is just like the one illustrated in Chapter 3 for measuring blank diameters.

You must remember also that the rings or skeleton reel seat have to be fitted on the grip before the butt cap or flared bottom section has been formed and glued on. If you're using flared cork, make a grip that is a ring or two short, and add and form these final rings in a separate operation after putting the rings or reel seat on the grip's shaft.

These are ¾-inch ID aluminum electrical conduit connectors, from which reel retaining rings can be made very easily. These connectors are formed by die-swaging, which compresses the metal and makes them rigid and very sturdy. The connector at left is in its original rough condition; the center connector has been wire-brushed on the bottom half; that on the right has been wire-brushed full length.

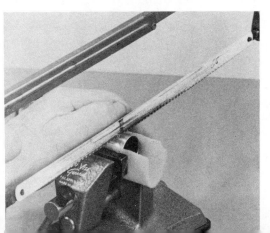

After wire-brushing, cut rings of the desired width from opposite ends of each connector; the ends are slightly flared.

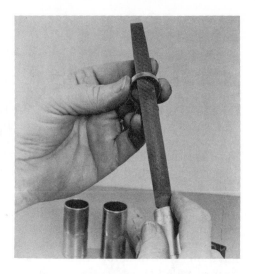

Smooth the saw burrs on the cut rims with a half-round fine-cut file.

Here are the finished rings on a section of cork grip. Remember, the cork must be filed and sanded flat along the plane of the rod's spine to ensure proper reel alignment.

GUIDE SPACING

Now we've reached the point of fitting guides. The types of spinning rod guides have been pretty well covered in earlier chapters, so let's assume that you've made up your mind as to the style of guide you'll use and get down to the brass tacks of spacing.

The size of the butt guide is all-important when fitting a spinning rod, as is its placement in relation to the face of the reel. The outside ring diameter of butt guides ranges from 25mm to 75mm. Except in the case of ceramic insert rings, the difference between the inside and outside diameters of these thin-ringed guides is so small that it can be ignored. Center guides range down to 6mm diameter, and tiptops have pretty well standardized ring diameters of 4mm to 8mm, but, like all tiptops, are sized by the inside diameter of their barrels.

Earlier, I noted that the function of the spinning rod's butt guide is to

A typical step-down in spinning guide sizes is pictured here; the guides go from a 30mm butt guide to a 20mm, 14mm, 10mm, two 8mm, and a 6mm guide just below the tiptop. However, as the following set of photos shows, size doesn't always govern guide selection.

reduce the funnel formed by the monofil as it pays off the reel, and to straighten it into a reasonably even line that will flow through the remaining guides with a minimum of friction. Reducing line friction means a more gradual step-down in size than is common to other types of rods. Between the butt guide and the guide above it, you can safely step down 10mm to 12mm in diameter from the butt guide to the second guide on heavy-duty rods and from 6mm to 8mm on lighter rods. On ultralight spinning rods that are used with very low-test monofil, you can go a bit further and step down as much as 16mm to 18mm between butt guide and second guide. Then, you can diminish diameters in three or four steps of 4mm to 6mm each to reduce the final guide to something close to the size of the ring in the tiptop.

Reducing generalities to specifics, you might use a 60mm ring as a butt guide on a heavy saltwater spinning rod; the guide above it would be 48mm to 50mm in diameter, the next guide would be about 36mm, and two guides above it would reduce in similar ratio. On a medium spinning rod the butt guide might be 30mm to 35mm, the second guide about 20mm, and so on down in diameter to an 8mm guide just below the tip.

While I was discussing the theory of rod design one day with Charlie Kewell, who was at that time in his 80s, and who'd worked at originating fishing tackle for more than 60 years, we got onto the subject of that compromise between friction and line slap that is the chief problem of anyone spacing guides on any rod. "If it comes to a choice," Charlie said thoughtfully, "I'd be inclined to put on one extra guide and accept the friction. You'll avoid straining your rod if you go that way, and at worst the friction of an extra guide will only cost you a very little bit of casting distance." Later, E. C. "Pop" Powell, the noted custom rod maker and designer, told me much the same thing in slightly different words. Both these men knew far more than most of us every learn about rod making, so I've always followed their advice.

According to the philosophy of these men, whose judgment I respect very much, most factory-fitted spinning rods and most of the charts I've seen giving spacings are at least one guide short. The only way to tell is by testing, so set the guides on your blank with masking tape according to the following charted suggestions and made the necessary test.

GUIDE SPACING FOR SPINNING RODS

(Moving either top guide or butt guide lower when making adjustments in spacing is not recommended.)

BLANK TYPE		ULTRALIGHT AND LIGHT		
LENGTH	5'	5$^1/_2$'	6'	6$^1/_2$'
GUIDES	4"–4$^1/_2$"	4"–4$^1/_2$"	4"–4$^1/_2$"	4"–4$^1/_2$"
SPACED	11"–12"	13"–14"	11"–12"	11"–12"
FROM TIP	19"–20"	23"–24"	20"–21"	22"–23"
	28"–29"	33"–34"	29"–30"	32"–33"
			34"–35"	45"–46"
BUTT GUIDE	24mm–26mm	24mm–26mm	26mm–28mm	26mm–28mm

BLANK TYPE		LIGHT AND MEDIUM-LIGHT		
LENGTH	6'	6$^1/_2$'	7'	7$^1/_2$'
GUIDES	4"–4$^1/_2$"	4"–4$^1/_2$"	4"–5"	4"–5"
SPACED	10"–11"	11"–12"	12"–13"	10"–11"
FROM TIP	19"–20"	21"–22"	24"–25"	20"–21"
	29"–30"	32"–33"	36"–37"	31$^1/_2$"–32$^1/_2$"
	40"–41"	46"–47"	51"–52"	44"–45"
				57"–58"
BUTT GUIDE	28mm–30mm	28mm–30mm	30mm–32mm	30mm–32mm

BLANK TYPE		MEDIUM-HEAVY	HEAVY	
LENGTH	8'	8$^1/_2$'	9'	10'
GUIDES	4$^1/_2$"–5"	4$^1/_2$"–5"	5"–5$^1/_2$"	5$^1/_2$"–6"
SPACED	13"–14"	13"–14"	15"–16"	17"–18"
FROM TIP	24"–25"	24"–25"	26"–27"	30"–31"
	35"–36"	37"–38"	39"–40"	45"–46"
	48"–49"	51"–52"	55"–56"	60"–61"
	63"–64"	68"–69"	71"–72"	77"–78"
BUTT GUIDE	34mm–36mm	34mm–36mm	46mm–50mm	60mm–70mm

TESTING

Remember, spacing suggestions in the chart are tentative and may need to be adjusted on the blank you're working on. Attach the guides to the blank with masking tape and try some practice casts. Watch the butt guide first for any indication that it is not doing its job of gathering the spiraling mono properly. By the way, you must make the practice casts with the same weight mono that you generally use, and the same reel. If you use two reels, test with both of them. After making a few lazy casts to get the feel of the new blank, try a few power casts and watch for tip vibration. We'll get to the cures for these two problems and also give you a second test in a later paragraph. Right now, our chief concern is line flow.

If the mono tends to foul on the butt guide, it's probably too close to the reel face. Don't move it until after you've made one more test that will be described later. Concentrate on the tip; if it vibrates, try a tiny bit of weight, as suggested in Chapter 5. Trim the tip only as a last resort, $^1/_2$ or $^3/_4$ inch at a time. When you're sure everything but the butt-guide problem is resolved, move on to the final test.

Set the reel drag at the point where you generally leave it. Attach a weight, a couple of pounds, to the line and lift the tip of the rod slowly— very slowly and carefully if the blank is graphite. You can lift a fiberglass blank as much as 45°, but don't lift the butt of a graphite blank more than 30° under a static load such as the deadweight you're using for this test.

First, check the path of the mono from the reel to the butt guide. It should barely touch the top of the guide's ring and go from the butt guide to the next guide in an almost straight line. If the mono's path isn't straight, fit a butt guide 2mm large in diameter. This should effectively solve your problem of the line piling up on the butt guide.

Next, with the rod at an angle—45° above horizontal for glass, 30° for graphite—check the distances between the bottom of the blank and the monofil, at the midpoint between guides. These should range from 2 to 3

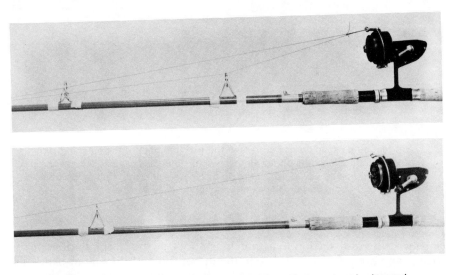

Shown in the top photo are two bad butt-guide settings on a spinning rod. The two guides are the same diameter. The top line path passes through the guide's center and will result in line slap and loss of casting distance. The line at the bottom is choked by the guide being too near the reel; this, too, will reduce casting distance. In the bottom photo the ideal butt-guide line path is shown, with the line just touching the top of the guide ring. No matter what the charts—including those in this book—say about spinning-rod guide spacing, be sure that the butt guide on the rod you're going to build is placed to achieve the line path shown in the bottom photo. Make this test with the reel and line you'll use on the rod, the reel's bail at the top.

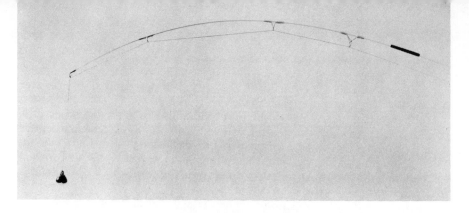

Here are other bad and good guide settings. In this photo, the bad spacing places too much strain on the rod's tip and will cause line slap when casting. There is far too much distance from tiptop to top guide, too much also to the next guide. See the next photo for the correct spacing.

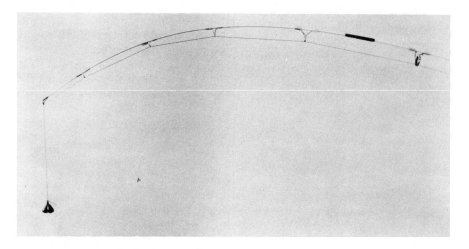

Correct guide spacing has corrected the bad line path of the spinning rod shown in the preceding photo. Here, an extra guide has been added and the topmost guide moved closer to the tip to create a line path that follows the rod's arc. In both photos, the same weight was used to stress the rod.

inches at the butt section to as much as 3 to 4 inches in the middle of the blank, and not more than 1 inch in the upper third. If the line-to-blank distances exceed these, you need to add another guide in order to get the most out of your rod. Add this guide in the section of the rod where the blade-to-line distances are the greatest and compensate by changing the spacing of all guides except the butt and top. Simply move the other guides, including the one you add, so that they are spaced evenly between the butt guide and the one next to the tiptop. This isn't especially scientific, but on the occasions when I've used the trick, it's worked.

When testing ultralight and light spinning rods that are fitted with shroud reel seats or keeper rings on the grip, make adjustments in guide

Spinning Rods

A **Ultralight:** Fenwick blank GSP661 (graphite); color, dark gray
Length: 5' 6'', 2-piece, 33½'' breakdown
Weight: Blank, ⅞ oz; fitted, 2 oz
Grip: Cork, straight
Reel seat: None, retaining rings
Guides: Aetna Foulproof set GT75
Winding: Gudebrod size A; primary gold metal #340; trim, underwound, black/yellow

B **Light:** Shakespeare blank #120336; white
Length: 7', 2-piece, 37'' breakdown
Weight: Blank: 2 oz; fitted, 4½ oz
Grip: Cork, straight
Reel seat: Featherweight 9SP skeleton
Guides: Butt, Allan ceramic CER; running, Mildrum stainless steel; top, Allan tungsten carbide
Winding: Gudebrod size A; primary gun metal #1011; trim black/white

C **Medium:** Lamiglas blank FW 965M; color, light amber
Length: 8', 2-piece, 48½'' breakdown
Weight: Blank, 3⅝ oz; fitted, 6⅝ oz
Grip: Cork, 3'' fore, 8'' butt
Reel seat: Varmac
Guides: Aetna Foulproof set GT21
Winding: Gudebrod size D; primary, gold metal #340; trim black #001

D **Medium-heavy:** Lamiglas blank GSH 962M (graphite); color, dark gray
Length: 8', 2-piece, 48¹/₂'' breakdown
Weight: Blank, 2⅞ oz; fitted, 4⅝ oz
Grip: Cork, straight, rubber butt cap
Reel seat: None, retaining rings
Guides: Aetna Foulproof set GT11
Winding: Gudebrod size A; primary orange #227; trim, underwound, black/orange varigated #8221, spiraled over gold Mylar between guide feet

E **Heavy:** Sabre blank #190-9; dark amber
Length: 9', 2-piece, 55½'' breakdown
Weight: Blank, 4⅜ oz; fitted, 9⅞ oz
Grip: Cork, 4'' fore, 9'' butt, rubber butt cap
Reel seat: Featherweight 9MS
Guides: Allan ceramic CEG series
Winding: Gudebrod size D; primary yellow #204 trim dark blue #245

105

spacing only after you've located the best spot along the grip for the reel, and only with the reel loaded with the test monofil you normally use. Don't worry about that future day when you'll get a new reel. Small-diameter monofil is very supple, and the chances are you'll need only to make a slight adjustment in the reel's location for everything to work perfectly.

Now, at this point you may well be wondering why you should take all this trouble testing when you can go to a store and buy a factory rod that seems to work pretty well with any reel, and without a lot of monkeying around setting guide spacings. The answer is simple. Guide spacings on these rods are computer-figured to give optimum average performance, and they do. Notice, not optimum performance, but optimum *average* performance. You pay 50 to 75 percent less for a factory rod than you would for a custom rod built to fit you and nobody else. That's the kind of rod you're making. You're paying for it with your own time and saving cash.

There are still a few more chores to be done before that blank can be called a spinning rod. One of them is winding on the guides. Choose a thread weight that won't overpower the blank, small diameter such as A for small ultralight blanks, heavier size C or D for medium-duty blanks, E for the big fellows. Directions for winding are in Chapter 3. So are those for applying the final touch, a protective finish over the windings.

Wind, varnish, and then go fishing with a rod that's uniquely your own.

7

Fly Rods

FLY FISHING IS a very ancient pastime and antedates the fly rod by fifteen or sixteen centuries. The first written reference to taking fish on a fly appeared about 200 A.D., while the modern fly rod dates back only to the 1790s. The first rods used for fly fishing were the all-purpose rods mentioned in the opening chapter; they were used for fishing worms and grubs and crickets—and probably liver and cheese as well, just as some fly rods are today.

The creator of the first bamboo fly rod was Thomas Regan, a veteran of the British Indian Army who found employment after his discharge from the service as a gillie, or gamekeeper, on a Scottish estate. Within a dozen years, however, there were a dozen or more rod makers at work in the British Isles, and in the 1850s the first American makers began practicing their craft.

A majority of the rods made in the early days were what would be called "soupy" by today's standards. Jim Payne, one of the great American makers and designers of custom rods, is credited with having originated the first of what were then called "dry-fly action" rods; this was in the early 1900s. During the dry-fly fever that swept the American angling world in the years that followed, other rod makers developed lighter, more responsive rods in both the dry-fly and wet-fly category. New lines appeared to match the rods. When fiberglass appeared in the late 1940s and graphite in the early 1970s, fresh avenues were opened to the rod maker, and there are other new materials that offer further possibilities for development in the future.

Fly rods still fall into the dry-fly and wet-fly categories. The former are characterized by fast tip action, the latter by a slower action that brings almost the entire length of the rod into play. Beginning in the 1950s, the late Leon P. Martuch pioneered the systems approach to fly fishing, and by the mid-1970s fly rods and fly rod blanks began to be classed not only by length and action, but by the weight of the line they were designed to handle most efficiently.

SELECTING THE BLANK

There are still fishermen who undervalue the need to match fly tackle not only in terms of rod and line, but in terms of the kind of water in which it is used. A fairy fly rod is a pleasure to use on a lake or in a stream with gentle currents, to drop a floating fly delicately on the surface. It's about as sensible to use a toothpick for a rod as to take one of these fairy wands out on a big, brawling river, or offshore to cast into the teeth of a brisk wind. Fast water and heavy currents or the long casts and big flies of saltwater angling call for scaled-up tackle. The motto of the fly rod fisherman and the rod maker might well transpose the saying, "Give me men to match my mountains" to "Give me rods to match my waters."

Your first consideration in choosing a fly rod blank should be determining where you're going to use the finished rod: on a limestone stream of the Eastern seaboard, a Southern lake, a Midwestern river with moderate currents, a Western steelhead river, or the ocean. You'll have no trouble finding a blank tailored to your exact needs and tastes. Some manufacturers list as many as sixty different fly rod blanks, in fiberglass and graphite, and even those whose selections aren't that comprehensive will typically offer from a dozen to twenty kinds of blanks.

Given this range of choice, you'll have no trouble selecting the rod that meets your requirements: a 6-foot blank on which to make a flea or fairy rod, an 8- or 8$\frac{1}{2}$-foot blank with fast or slow action, a 9- or 9$\frac{1}{2}$-foot blank for steelhead or saltwater fishing. As this is being written, the long rod seems to be making a comeback after a long period when anglers' enthusiasm was directed toward short rods. Once more fly rod users are discovering that rods in the 9-foot plus class are no more tiring to cast than those of 7$\frac{1}{2}$ or 8 feet, and are a lot more efficient in reducing line drag when dry-fly fishing. They also give the user a better feel and a greater degree of line control in all styles of fly rod angling.

Some of this rediscovery can be credited to lighter long blanks of graphite. When I began to retire my bamboo fly rods and switch to fiberglass, I was a bit startled to discover that the new glass rods were heavier in 9-foot lengths than were double-built bamboos in the same length. This didn't inhibit me from using them, of course. I made up 10-foot fiberglass fly rods with butt extensions for steelhead fishing and 10- to 11$\frac{1}{2}$-foot two-hand fly rods for use in saltwater. But while these long, heavy rods had their place, most of my heavy-water fly rod fishing was done with a 9-foot 3-inch job made on a Fenwick blank that I found pleasant to handle.

A bit of advice, then, on heavy rods. Any fly rod 9 feet or longer should be fitted with an extension butt, even if the extension is quite short, 4 inches or so. The extension allows you to rest the rod butt in your midsection without interfering with your use of the reel. And, unless you're willing to learn how to handle a two-hand salmon fly rod, which calls for a casting technique different from that of the one-hand rod, confine your field to rods with this easier, more conventional grip. With the advent of graphite blanks, the two-hand salmon fly rod is coming back, however. If you're inclined to experiment, and fish water where extra-long casts are needed, you'd probably enjoy using one.

Whatever your choice of blank, the procedures followed in converting a fly rod blank into a working rod are essentially the same basic methods covered in Chapter 3. We might look at the differences, though, for there are some.

FERRULES

Give thought to using mini- or micro-ferrules if you're making a rod on a blank that's 7 feet or shorter. They result in a little less weight and logically on light rods should reduce the flat spot any ferrule creates. These spots are more noticeable on light and ultralight rods than on heavier ones. Glass-to-glass ferrules should be confined to light and ultralight rods. Fly rods are subject to a lot more flexes per fishing day than other types, and for all their streamlined virtue, glass-to-glass ferrules may bell at the mouth of the female or socket joint under long, continued use.

Replacing these ferrules is a somewhat tedious job. If the male ferrule has to be replaced, it must be drilled out and the inner wall of the blank scraped clean. If the female joint bells, it must be trimmed and then the plug reworked to fit. If you use this method of ferruling on a fly rod, there are two materials you can use to reinforce the rim of the socket, both of which are fitted in the same way. One is a ring about $1/4$ inch wide cut from the end of a ferrule of the proper diameter. The other, which costs a bit less, comes in the form of thin-walled brass tubing, available in 12-inch lengths, in outside diameters graduated in 32nds of an inch from $1/16$ to $1/2$ inch. In all this tubing the wall thickness is uniform, .014 inch, or approximately $1/64$ inch. You need only measure the outside diameter of the blank at the point where you want to place the ring and add $1/64$ inch to allow for the tubing's wall thickness to determine the outside diameter of the tubing you buy. Cut off one end to make a ring of the width you want, and then fit it with epoxy at the socket's rim. Hardware stores generally have this tubing in stock; if you can't find it locally, order from Brookstone Co., whose address will be found in Appendix 3.

Naturally, when you're winding the rod, you'll cover the reinforcing ring with a wrap. The pictures show the steps in fitting this ring to your blank.

Any rod—but most especially any fly rod—that you have fitted with glass-to-glass ferrules should be reinforced at the end of the female ferrule joint. Do this with a ring of metal cut from the brass tubing discussed in the text, or with a ring cut from a ferrule of proper inside diameter. The ring should be glued at the joint with epoxy.

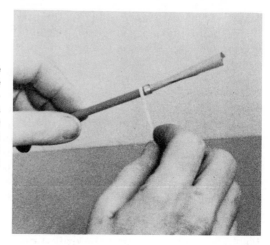

When using epoxy or any adhesive or liquid such as color preservative or varnish at the very rim of a ferrule, protect the open end with a roll of paper stuck into it. When the epoxy used to set the reinforcing ring begins to set up, taper it with a toothpick from the blade to the ring to make winding easier.

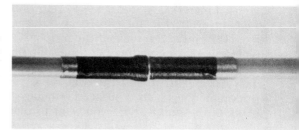

When wrapped, your glass-to-glass ferrule joint should look like this—just a thin strip of the reinforcing ring visible between the butt and tip section winds.

GRIPS AND REEL SEATS

After the blank has been ferruled, fit the grip. On fly rods, of course, the reel seat is below the grip. If you're making a very lightweight rod, you may want to use a cork reel seat, formed integrally with the grip and fitted with keeper rings. Except for the smaller diameter, forming a fly rod reel seat of this kind is exactly like forming one for a spinning rod grip, as detailed in Chapter 6. Small-diameter rings can be cut from skill aluminum tubing or from the electrical conduit referred to there. Or, if you're unable to find conduit in other than full-length pieces, retaining rings for a fly rod cork reel seat can be cut from conduit connectors, which are made of polished aluminum and are available with a $3/4$-inch inside diameter. Be sure to groove the reel seat when making a grip of this kind, to accommodate the reel's foot.

Template patterns for forming fly rod grips are included in this chapter; for instructions on using them, see Chapter 6. You have the option of using a preformed cork grip, if you like any of the three or four contours in which these are available. Some preformed grips can be worked down to a different contour, if you wish. A fly rod, by the way, lends itself ideally to the customizing touch of a thumbprint mentioned in Chapter 3, because of the thumb's position on the grip when casting.

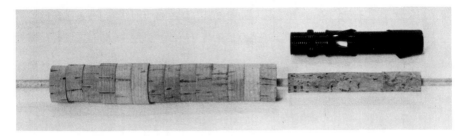

Here are the components for a fly rod grip: cork rings, reel-seat bushings, and reel seat. Notice the three rings just to the left of center in the line of corks, which are slightly larger in outside diameter than the other corks. As the grip will bulge out at this point, the larger rings will make it easier to form.

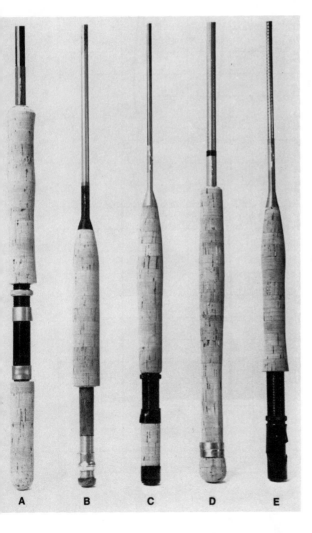

Variations in fly rod grips: (**A**) full Wells grip with removable extension butt, on a 9½-foot Scientific Anglers graphite rod blank; (**B**) Payne grip with wrapped winding check and reversed wooden center reel seat on a 6-foot Fenwick blank; (**C**) Phillipe cigar with wrapped winding check and locking cork reel seat on a 7-foot ultralight Lamiglas graphite blank; (**D**) Phillipe comfort grip with full cork retainer-ring reel seat on an 8½-foot Lamiglas fiberglass blank; (**E**) Hardy grip with wound winding check on an 8-foot Shakespeare graphite blank. Broadly speaking, the grip fitted to a fly rod blank should have some relationship to the rod's weight and length.

A   B   C   D   E

TEMPLATE PATTERNS FOR FLY-ROD GRIPS

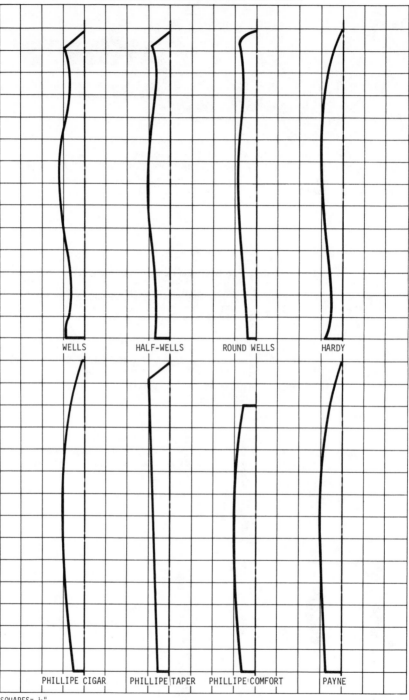

WELLS   HALF-WELLS   ROUND WELLS   HARDY

PHILLIPE CIGAR   PHILLIPE TAPER   PHILLIPE COMFORT   PAYNE

SQUARES= ½"

SELECTING GUIDES

Choosing guides for a fly rod is a very straightforward matter. The butt, or stripping guide, can be a ring guide of tungsten carbide, or, better yet, a ceramic insert guide. A second ring guide above the stripper guide is almost a must on fly rods in the 9-foot class, and a good idea on rods down to 7 or 7½ feet. Remember, about 40 percent of damage to fly lines can be blamed on scored or pitted butt guides, and 60 percent on rough tiptops. Ceramic insert guides at both butt and tiptop will soon pay for themselves in reducing line wear as well as friction.

On rods using lines smaller than weight 6, an 8mm butt guide is adequate; for lines from weight 6 to 8, use a 10mm butt guide; for lines above 9, the butt guide should be 12mm. The second guide can be the same size as the stripper, or one size smaller. Snake guides, which are fitted above the stripper and second guide, are sized by number, #7 being the largest. They step down to #1, then to 1/0 and down to the tiniest, 4/0, for use on fairy rods.

With the appearance of the single-foot, lightweight ceramic insert guides that require only a single narrow winding, a new dimension may be opening up for flycasters. I say "may," because at the time this is being written these guides are still too new to be evaluated with accuracy or fairness. Going by the book, they should eliminate line cling, which is often a problem with heavy wet-fly lines, and should reduce friction as well. Things don't always go by the book in fishing, as every angler knows, but if you make up a heavy-duty fly rod, these guides ought to be worth trying. Most dealers have them in stock.

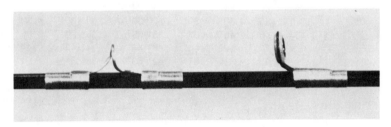

Conventional snake guide, left, and single-foot ceramic insert guide for fly rods. The single-foot guide, relatively recent in origin, requires only one winding and holds the line above the blade. It is best for heavy-duty rods.

While a looped tiptop is traditionally fitted to fly rods, the trend is to braced tiptops with ceramic inserts. I'm inclined to stay with the lightweight loop tiptop on rods of up to 8 feet, but on heavier rods, especially 9-foot rods used in big-water fishing with monofil backing that's often stripped off the reel by a big fish, I'd go to the braced ceramic insert tiptop. All tiptops are sized in 64ths of an inch, the measurement being the inside diameter of the barrel.

GUIDE SPACING

Smooth line flow is very important in fly fishing, especially when you're shooting for long casts with a weight-forward taper line or shooting head. Bringing into action the full strength of the rod is important; so is protecting the rod's delicate tip. However, proper line spacing is perhaps easier to achieve on a fly rod than on any other type. As you'll see from the chart, there's a consistent pattern to fly rod guide spacing for both fast-tip or dry-fly rods and another for slow-action or wet-fly rods. You can follow the same patterns regardless of line weight or rod weight and get the greatest casting efficiency and smoothest line flow.

As in the case of the previous charts, don't take this one as gospel. Your first impression is going to be that there are too many guides, but I've found that with too few guides the risk of line cling increases, and I would much rather accept the small increase in guide friction than the major problem of cling. Snake guides must be spaced more closely than they are on many rods to overcome both cling and line wobble. Using $8\frac{1}{2}$- and 9-foot rods with the chart spacing, I've never had any difficulty in making

GUIDE SPACING FOR FLY RODS

BLANK ACTION LENGTH	6'	6½	7	7½	FAST TIP (DRY FLY) 8	8½	9'
GUIDES	3″	3″	3″	3″	3″–3½″	3″–3½″	3″–3½″
SPACED	8″	8″	8″	8″	8″–8½″	8″–8½″	8″–8½″
FROM TIP	13″	13″	13″	13″	13″–13½″	13″–13½″	13″–13½″
	18″	18″	18″	18″	18″–18½″	18″–18½″	18″–18½″
	24″	26″	24″	24″	24″–24½″	24″–24½″	24″–24½″
	31″	35″	30″	30″	30″–30½″	30″–30½″	30″–30½″
	40″	45″	40″	37″	38″–39″	38″–39″	37″–37½″
				52″	44″	44″–45″	44″–44½″
					48″–49″	50″–51″	51″–51½″
					62″–63″	60″–61″	57″–57½″
						70″–71″	66″–67″
							74″–75″

BLANK ACTION LENGTH	7'	7½	MEDIUM/SLOW (WET FLY) 8'	8½'	9'
GUDIES	3″	3″	3″	3″	3″
SPACED	7″	7″	7″	7″	7″
FROM TIP	11″	11″	11″	11″	11″
	16″–17″	16″–17″	16″–17″	16″–17″	16″–17″
	22″–23″	22″–23″	22″–23″	22″–23″	22″–23″
	29″–30″	29″–30″	29″–30″	29″–30″	29″–30″
	38″–39″	38″–39″	38″–39″	38″–39″	38″–39″
	51″–52″	44″–45″	44″–45″	47″–48″	47″–48″
		57″–58″	52″–53″	56″–57″	56″–57″
			63″–64″	70″–71″	66″–67″
					76″–77″

(Last guide shown is butt or stripper guide)

Fly Rods

A **Ultralight** (#5 or #6 line): Fenwick blank FL 726; color, amber
Length: 6' 6", 2-piece, 38" breakdown, glass-to-glass ferrules
Weight: Blank, 1½ oz; fitted, 2⁹/₁₆ oz
Grip: Payne, wound grip-check
Reel seat: Maple center, made from Allan #50568; fixed hood inverted
Guides: Agate stripping, gold snake running, Varmac ceramic top
Winding: Gudebrod size A; primary beige #832; trim brown #396

B **Ultralight** (#2 or #3 line): Lamiglas blank GF 84 (graphite); color, grey
Length: 7', 2-piece, 43" breakdown, factory ferruled
Weight: Blank, ¹¹/₁₆ oz; fitted, 2⅛ oz
Grip: Phillipe Cigar, wound grip-check
Reel seat: Cork center, made from Allan #50098
Guides: Fuji BMH series
Winding: Gudebrod size A; primary gun metal #1011; trim, overwound, gray #602

C **Light** (#7 or #8 line): Shakespeare blank #120274 (graphite); color, black
Length: 8', 2-piece, 49" breakdown, factory ferruled
Weight: Blank, 1³/₁₆ oz; fitted, 3 oz
Grip: Hardy, wound grip check
Reel seat: Allan #50098
Guides: Fuji BMH stripping and top, black chrome snake running
Winding: Gudebrod size A; primary gray #602; trim, overwound, black/white varigated #8002

D **Medium** (#7 or #8 line): Lamiglas blank 96-7S; color, amber
Length: 8', 2-piece, 49½" breakdown, factory ferruled
Weight: Blank, 2½ oz; fitted, 3¾ oz
Grip: Phillipe cigar
Reel seat: Cork, retaining rings
Guides: Varmac ceramic AT series stripping and top; Aetna Foulproof running
Winding: Gudebrod size D; primary golden-rod #209; trim orange #221

long casts. Of course, you must use snake guides big enough to allow free line flow—and this means guides no smaller than 3/0 in the top three or four positions of a 9-foot rod.

Reminding you to fit a reel to the blank you're testing may seem to be unnecessary, but when I first began making rods it was the habit of all fishermen to remove lines from the reels and transfer them to storage reels if they were going to be unused for any length of time. The silk lines of that time made this necessary. Laziness and lack of understanding prompted me to test my first few fly rods without reels on them, using the line direct from the storage reel, from which I stripped enough line to use for the tests. Later, the rods proved to be out of balance just enough to make using them unpleasant. Resetting the guides with a reel on the rod cured this, but it took me twice as long to get a good job as would have been the case if I'd used a reel in my first tests.

There's a much closer relationship between the fly rod and its line and reel than exists in other styles of fishing. The reel, acting as a truncated pendulum in casting, can add power to a rod or keep it from developing its maximum thrust. If you encounter problems in getting a rod-line-reel balance, there are a number of cures. A slight change in butt-guide spacing makes a difference, as does switching to a lighter or heavier reel. Some fly reels have a cavity in their axles into which split shot can be placed to add weight to them.

While modern lines are well designed and accurate in their weighting, you might find it necessary to snip off a few inches of its front taper to get the line to turn over properly. A blank's unsatisfactory performance is seldom traceable to the line, however. It can usually be found in the butt-guide spacing or the reel weight.

WINDINGS

Windings are another factor that will affect a rod's performance. Quite a number of years ago, I fished for a few days with an English-made rod that followed the old traditional British pattern of winding. This pattern was established in the early days of the bamboo rod, when the material's characteristics were still being explored, and when glues and varnishes were less reliable than they now are. Pioneer British rod makers started winding the entire length of their rods in spirals or with narrow trim strips, not as much for decoration as to keep the strips from parting if glue or varnish gave way. The rod I used was relatively new in spite of its traditional winding, but its erratic and slow action made using it anything but a pleasure. The fellow who'd loaned me the rod was not only my host, but a comparative stranger, so I didn't complain, but that experience instilled into me a deep distrust of overwound rods.

Fiberglass and graphite rods don't need extra windings and shouldn't be burdened with them. When an inch or more of closely spaced, tightly wound thread is added to each side of a guide, a flat spot equal to that caused by a ferrule can be created. When such windings are over-wrapped with another layer of thread, the effect is compounded. You'll get the best performance of which a blank is capable if you burden it with the least amount of excess baggage. Appearances are deceitful. You'll see many factory rods that look overwound, but remember that in almost all cases the windings are computer-designed, applied under carefully controlled machine tension, and their effect on the blank calculated into the design.

These are factors the individual rod maker can't allow for unless he has access to a computer and the skill to program it. So, don't take factory rods as prototypes. The blanks in a factory must be finished into rods on the basis of average spacings, windings, guides, and other fittings. As noted earlier, the plant turning out several thousand rods a week can't stop to test each individual blank in the painstaking way that you can. The manufacturer is investing money in wages; you're just working for the pleasure of making a rod that's tailored to your own needs, and you'll get your reward from using it.

8

Split-Bamboo Rods

ONE OF THE STRANGEST aspects of the fishing tackle industry for a score of years has been that while fine bamboo rods are in greater demand than ever, the material from which they're made and the number of craftsmen capable of turning them out dwindled almost to the point of extinction. The number of custom bamboo rod makers is now increasing, though prices on their finished products are rising. A good bamboo rod will now cost you from $150 to $350 without a spare tip, and $225 to $450 with the extra tip that ensures you against crippling damage and makes a butt section useless.

Bamboo supplies have increased but are still not plentiful. Bamboo as a rod material virtually disappeared during the 1940s, when China was ravaged by war, The finest Tonkin cane came from a small area in two Chinese provinces, Kwangtung and Kwangsi, where it was harvested from mountaintops over which high winds blew and toughened the canes as they matured. A trickle of bamboo began to come to the United States during the 1950s, via India and England, and the trickle has grown, but not to a flood. Custom rod makers have standing orders for virtually 100 percent of all the Tonkin cane harvested, so you as an individual wanting to make one or two rods would be hard-pressed indeed to get hold of the few stalks of raw bamboo you'd need.

Don't confuse rod-quality cane with ordinary bamboo. The kind of bamboo rod makers use consists of 3-to 5-inch diameter sections 8 or 9 feet long. From these, after careful inspection by experts, strips are sawn lengthwise, and from these strips come the smaller strips which are in time formed into bamboo blanks. In the early days of rod making, the big cane sections were split by hand, following the bamboo's natural grain, which gave the first bamboo rods their old name, "riven and glued fishing rods,"

Bamboo is actually a species of grass and is widely distributed around the world. It will grow in a variety of climates but favors warm areas. The Tonkin cane from which rods are made has unusually thick walls with a greater number of longitudinal fibers growing under a hard, enamellike shell that forms the outside surface. The shell and fibers beneath are the only part of the stalk that are used in rod making, since below them a soft layer of pith makes up the rest of the wall. In a section of bamboo 3 to 5 inches in diameter, the walls will be 1 to 2 inches thick, of which as little as $^1/_4$ to $^5/_8$ inches of the outside portion is all that can be used for a rod.

PREPARING THE BAMBOO

Though I have no recent information on this point, I assume that today's Tonkin canes are still cured in the traditional manner. After harvesting, the canes are cut into sections 8 to 9 feet long; a stalk 20 feet long will yield only one section. These sections are then split in one lengthwise cut to expose the interior pith, and are then buried in lime-filled pits for two years. The lime removes most of the moisture from the pith during this time. The sections are bundled and shipped after this preliminary aging or curing, but the curing still is not complete. The rod maker who receives the bamboo stacks it in heated sheds, where it will rest for another two or three years and dry still further before being used.

When totally dry, the bamboo sections are sawed lengthwise into wide strips and the inner walls carefully scraped to remove all pith. Almost all the strength and resilience of bamboo lies in its outer shell and the fibers directly below it; the shell itself is only a few hundredths of an inch thick, the fibers less than $^1/_2$ inch. The outer shell has a natural coating something like varnish that is stripped away, and the bumpy joints, called nodes, are filed smooth. The strips are then tempered by exposure to direct heat and while still hot are straightened. When worked hot, bamboo retains the shape into which it is fixed, so the strips cool in straight-grained lengths, the grain, of course, being the inner fibers.

Mechanization did not come to bamboo rod making until the 1930s, with the development of milling machines equipped with tungsten carbide blades that could cut tapers with 1/1000th of an inch precision. Before that, the strips were split and planed by hand in long V-blocks of hardwood or metal that were milled to 60° angles. The rod maker made a few passes with his plane, forming angle and taper, on one side, turned the strip and made a few on the other side, until the angle was formed and the taper established. Great care was required not to damage the outer shell, which is what forms the surface of a bamboo rod.

With their taper and angle formed, the strips were then glued together to form a hexagonal-shaped blank, with the spots where the nodes had been removed carefully staggered so that no two would fall in the same place. The strips were then glued and wrapped with spirals of string, one wound from the left, the other from the right, until the glue set. This was to ensure that the blank would dry straight. The finished blank was then cleaned and polished, ferrules set, and the other steps completed to turn it into a rod.

Today, the same processes are followed except that the long job of hand-planing the strips is no longer required; a milling machine does this. However, the remainder of the work is done by hand. A new step has been added, that of resin-impregnation. A flexible resin compound is used that flows into the spaces between the fibers, surrounding them and prolonging their useful life, and stabilizing the rod's action.

If you were to decide today to make a bamboo rod blank from scratch, and could find the Tonkin cane from which to make it, your first job would be to make the necessary planing block with its 60° slots that establish the taper of the strips from butt to tip. You can do this, if you take on the job, with gunsmiths' checkering tools and riffling files. Early rod makers fashioned their own planing blocks, and what man has done once, he can do again. The planing block is the essential requirement; apart from a small block plane, the only other tools you'd need would be those used in converting a fiberglass or graphite blank into a rod.

If you yearn for a brand-new bamboo rod of your own making, the easy way to go is to buy a blank or kit. The custom bamboo rod makers selling these are all listed in Appendix 3. Orvis is the only one I'm sure sells kits, which run about 25 percent below the cost of one of their finished bamboo rods and include all components as well as a booklet giving instructions on such things as guide spacing. Winston, Rod & Reel, and Midland Tackle all sell bamboo blanks and components. Send for their catalogs and decide which one offers the kind of blank you're looking for. You'll find a wide choice of fly rod blanks in lengths from 6 to 9 feet and with fast, medium, and slow actions. The same procedures followed in making up a rod on a graphite or fiberglass blank apply to bamboo; any additional details will be found in this chapter.

REFURBISHING BAMBOO RODS

If you have a chance to buy an old bamboo rod that needs a bit of refurbishing, do so. Rods by some of the master craftsmen of the past are very valuable today. Look for signatures like Payne, C. F. Orvis, Mills, E. C. Powell, Gillum, Wes Jordan, Garrison, Young, Thomas. Any time you devote to rebuilding a still-usable bamboo rod made by one of these masters will be well spent, for examples of their work are at this writing selling for $200 to $500 or more. In judging the value of a used rod, keep in mind that bamboo rods have a service life of between 2,000 and 2,500 days of continuous casting, or about eight years of fishing every day from dawn to dusk. Few used rods have seen this kind of service, and those which have will show it by the sagging feel they have when false-cast. If an old rod still feels alive and springy, you can probably refurbish it and use it for several years.

If the rod has a set in it, this can be removed after the old varnish has been stripped away. Don't use a varnish remover, but carefully scrape off the old finish with a cabinetmaker's flat-edge scraper, being careful not to nick the walls. When taking off the old guides and wrappings, observe this same precaution. Slice into the windings from one end, cutting only two or three threads deep, and unwind them rather than cutting them away. Use a plastic mesh scouring pad, never metal, to finish cleaning up the surface of the bamboo.

Remove sets by holding the bent portion of the rod section over the spout of a boiling kettle for three or four minutes—the time will vary with the diameter of the area on which you're working—moving the area to be straightened up and down in the steam. Then very carefully flex the area

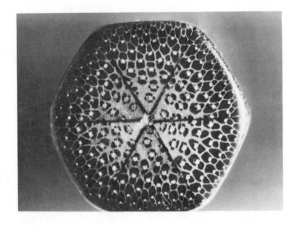

This photo shows the fiber structure and glue-lines of an impregnated bamboo blank. Notice how thin the outer shell is, and how the pith increases at the center. *Courtesy of The Orvis Company.*

This is the correct way to remove the old varnish from a bamboo fly rod section: with a flat-blade cabinet scraper drawn carefully along the flats of the rod.

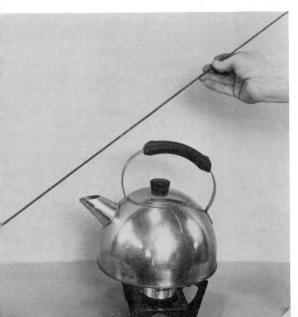

To prepare a bamboo rod section for removing a set, or slight curve, steam it over a teakettle spout for several minutes, moving it up and down in the steam.

Then, gently flex the section against the curve and hold it in this position until the bamboo cools. More than one steam-and-flex treatment may be required if the set is pronounced.

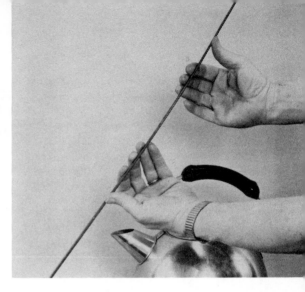

that's crooked in your fingertips, flexing against the bend. You may have to repeat the operation two or three times before it's straightened. Be careful not to twist a bamboo rod at any time. Bamboo is very sensitive to twisting and careless handling in this respect, even while jointing or unjointing a rod, may cause the inner fibers to shear off.

Damaged grips and dented or worn ferrules can be replaced on bamboo rods just as they would be on fiberglass or graphite. Just scrape away old adhesive carefully, without nicking the thin outer shell. Winding and all other procedures follow the ones detailed elsewhere for the different rebuilding operations.

Unlike modern synthetic rod blank materials, bamboo must be protected against moisture with a thin coat of varnish. And let me emphasize "thin." Thick coats of varnish will spoil the action of a bamboo rod—or of any other rod, for that matter. Before winding or varnishing, polish the surface of a bamboo rod with felt pads. Cut these from an old hat or felt bedroom slippers and moisten them for the first cleaning operation, then finish polishing with dry pads.

Warm varnish that you're going to use on a rod, putting the can in a pan of water and not over direct heat. Coat the windings first, using first your fingertip and then a brush for a final coat. When the windings are dry, apply a very thin coating to the entire length of the rod, using your fingers like squeegees to get the thinnest possible coat. Fill in the spots under the guides and the voids where the windings go over the guide feet with a brush or a toothpick. Unless these spots are protected, moisture will get in and not only discolor the winding thread, but perhaps also enter the hairline crack left when the rod was glued. If you get a drop of varnish on a guide, remove it with crocus cloth. Nothing will score a line like a scrap of dry varnish on a guide.

Let the varnish dry thoroughly, a day or even two, with the rod in a dust-free, lint-free atmosphere. Then give the surface a light rubbing with a dry felt pad and apply a second thin varnish coat. The thinner you can put it on, the better. When the final coat has dried, you're at last ready to use your "new" bamboo rod.

9

Special-Purpose Freshwater Rods

OVER THE YEARS a number of special types of rods have evolved to fit the needs of anglers who seek fish under special conditions. For the most part, these rods are useful only when the conditions that brought them into being exist. Their use may be limited by geography, either water or climatic conditions or the limited distribution of a fish species. Or, the rods may be designed for portability, or for use with a special kind of lure. In this chapter, we'll take a look at the construction of these special kinds of rods.

Pack or travel rods are the most common special-purpose rods. They are designed to be highly portable, in a backpack or a suitcase, or strapped to the luggage carrier of a trail bike. The rod may be built on a baitcast/spincast, spinning, or fly rod blank; perhaps the most often used are short spinning rod blanks $6^{1}/_{2}$ to $7^{1}/_{2}$ feet long.

Convertible rods are not as common as they were at one time; increasing angler sophistication has led many fishermen to question the convertibility concept. It is possible, however, to make up a rod that can be used equally well for fly and spin casting as we will see later on.

Ice rods are often called "jig rods" now, and have migrated to the South from the upper Midwestern area where lakes freeze over. They are very short rods, often little more than a grip and an 8- or 10-inch stub of blank. They were never intended for casting; their use is limited to dancing a bait or feathered lead-head jig on the bottom directly below the rod tip.

Muskie rods and their close cousins, popping rods, are beefed-up versions of baitcast/spincast rods. The muskie rod originated in the lakes of the Upper Midwest many years ago, when regular baitcasting rods proved too fragile to handle the big baits and lures offered to this hard-jawed freshwater giant, or to hold the fish if it took the offering. The popping rod is a stretched-out, dieted version of the muskie rod, with a stiff tip action, generally associated with surface baits in Southern and Southwestern waters.

We've already covered the heavy-duty fly rods used in saltwater fishing; they're little different from other fly rods except for their enlarged dimensions. We will take a closer look at the two-hand salmon fly rod, which is undergoing a revival of popularity, and go into details of its design. Surf spinning rods and other saltwater rods will be found in later chapters.

Finally, we'll pay a little attention to a new kind of rod that has appeared on the angling scene. This is a very long, very soft-action rod originated in the Great Lakes steelhead area for the purpose of taking these big, tough fighters on exceptionally light lines. This whippy rod began life under the name of the "bike rod," but its originator has re-named it the "maxi-rod."

All these specialty rods can be made on blanks that are readily available except for the maxi-rod. All of them, including the latter, can be built up by following the basic procedures already detailed in Chapter 3 and elsewhere in the book. The purpose of this chapter is to investigate certain aspects of the construction of these rods that call for special attention.

PACK RODS

Rods of this type antedate the use of bamboo; a few specimens of solid wooden English-made pack rods of the late 1700s survive as museum pieces. At least one of them I've seen had what today would be called "glass-to-glass" ferrules, except that these were "wood-to-wood." A band of engraved German silver was fitted to the blade at each jointing point, the ferrules tapered quite sharply where they fitted together, and from a hole in the bottom of the male ferrule a peg of the wood from which the rod was made protruded to mate with a hole in the top of the female ferrule. The rod broke down into five 24-inch sections and when jointed was 12 feet long.

Modern pack or travel rods are much shorter, usually in the $6^1/_2$- to $7^1/_2$-foot range, and break into four or five sections, each 18 to 22 inches long. Medium-action spinning rod blanks are favored for pack rods, and some are fitted with reversible grips so that they can be used with both fly and spinning reels. Others have grips built up on a section of fiberglass cut from an old rod and fitted with a shroud reel seat or keeper rings. A separate grip made this way will add about 10 inches to a short blank. The butt of a rod that has a separate grip must be fitted with a male ferrule, with the female set flush into the top of the grip. A chuck grip can also be used.

Let me discourage you from building a pack rod with sections shorter than 18 inches. When section length is reduced beyond this point, in an effort to make a shorter, more compact rod for carrying, the action almost invariably suffers. Even if a light, thin-walled blank is used, inserting four ferruled joints less than 18 inches apart will create flat spots and give the rod a jerky action.

Nor would I suggest that you use a blank shorter than $5^1/_2$ feet for a pack rod, unless it is to be fitted with a separate grip. When you fit an integral grip to such a short rod, it must be cut into 15-inch sections, and by the time you add a couple of ferrules you'll have a rod that won't really give you much pleasure. If you cut a 5-foot rod into only two sections, and center-ferrule it, then the sections are too long to fit most suitcases, though such a rod would be fine for backpacking.

To ensure the best action from a pack rod, fit it with micro-ferrules.

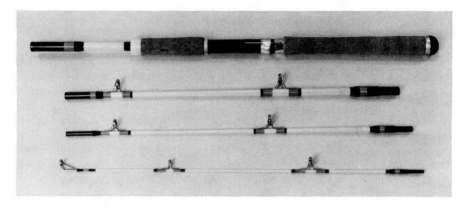

A travel rod typically is broken down into four sections, each 18 to 22–24 inches long. This rod is heavier than most pack or travel rods; it was designed for light trolling and baitfishing in salt water and in big freshwater lakes.

These reduce the area of flatness that long ferrules create. Of course, your pack rod must begin with a one-piece blank, if you want to tailor the rod to your own dimensions. Fenwick's catalog lists the only factory-ferruled rod blanks offered, but does not list the length of the sections. From them you can get your choice of an 8-foot graphite and three fiberglass pack rod blank sets.

Assuming that you're beginning with a one-piece blank, first mark the cut lines. To save you time, the chart that follows gives the most common section lengths and indicates how far from the butt each cut must be made.

NUMBER OF SECTIONS	LENGTH OF BLANK*	LENGTH OF SECTIONS	DISTANCE OF CUTS FROM BUTT OF BLANK		
3	5¹/₂'	22"	22"	44"	
4	6'	18"	18"	36"	54"
4	6¹/₂'	19¹/₂"	19¹/₂"	39"	58¹/₂"
4	7'	21"	21"	42"	63"
5	7¹/₂'	18"**	14"	32"	50"

*Length of blank = length of finished rod if grip is fitted as part of butt section; if detached grip is fitted, divide length of blank into equal lengths.
**Except for butt section, which is shortened to 14" to increase length of upper sections and improve rod action.

After determining the length of the sections and marking the cut lines, find the blank's spine as detailed in Chapter 3. Mark its location not only at the tip and butt, but at each cut line. Be sure these markings are long enough to show above and below the ferrules.

When the blank has been cut and fitted with ferrules, use the chart in Chapter 6 to get approximate guide spacing. Remember, this will only give you a starting point. Test the spacings as described in that chapter and shift them if necessary to get the best action from the blank.

For pack rods that will be fitted for use with both monofil and fly lines, you'll have to do a lot of compromising that can only be determined after you've tested the blank with both. Quite frankly, I consider the spinning rod/fly rod combination a compromise that's almost unworkable. The differences in the requirements of these two kinds of rods are so great that you're going to wind up with a rod that won't be totally satisfactory for either spinning or fly fishing. You'd be better off making up two separate blanks.

Finally, be sure to carry your pack rod in a case. Whether it's going to be packed in a knapsack or on the luggage carrier of a bike or in a suitcase, the tip and guides need protection. You can make a case quite easily in ten minutes, at a cost of a couple of bucks. Buy a piece of 2-inch diameter aluminum tubing, of the necessary length from your local hardware store, plumber, or sheet metal shop. Order a pair of rubber butt caps from any of the several mail-order tackle supply houses who list them in their catalogs. Strangely, these caps are seldom stocked by local tackle shops. They cost less than $1.00 a pair. Just fit the caps over the ends of the tubing to make your rod case. It will let you travel without worrying about the fate of your rod.

COMBINATION RODS

Combination rods, intended to be used interchangeably for spin and fly fishing, are somewhat like ostrich eggs, in that you don't see one very often. These rods are generally found in the hands of purists who refuse to accept the compromise necessary when the same rod with a change in reel positions is used for both types of angling. The distinction between the combination rod and the pack rod is that the combination offers two tips, one for fly, the other for spinning. Occasionally, these rods will be made up as pack rods as well as combination rods.

Normally, though, a combination rod will have one butt section with a reversible grip or a grip fitted with retainer rings to allow use of the fly reel at the bottom and the spinning reel higher on the grip. Occasionally a shroud reel seat will be fitted. To make one you'll need a pair of blanks with compatible diameters at the point where they are to be ferruled. Because no pair of blanks is precisely the same as another, there are absolutely no rules to go by, not even rules of thumb. You'll just have to experiment with each blank, using guides held on with masking tape, until you discover the best combination of ferruling points and guide spacings.

A few observations might be helpful, even without rules, Get blanks with the same type of action, either fast tip or progressive taper, so that the butt action will be compatible with each of the tips. Use the fly rod blank for the butt section; uniformity of action is more important when flycasting than when spincasting. Use a smaller butt guide than you would normally select for a spinning rod. You'll generally be fishing light-test mono on such a rod, and it'll flow easily through a guide smaller than you'd fit on a straight spinning rod. The smaller guide won't appreciably affect spincasting and will keep the fly line from getting snarled in the butt guide.

Don't be discouraged if you wind up with tips of different lengths. It's fairly common to vary tip lengths of combination rods in order to get the best action from each tip, and it's sometimes impossible to do this and maintain uniform ferrule settings. You may have to try several ferrules before discovering the right combination.

Keep in mind all the ways you can use to alter a blank's performance and be prepared to use any or all of them to get a well-behaved rod. They include weighting the tip with lead wire, using different kinds of guides, and trimming either the tip or the butt a fraction of an inch at a time. You might find that a combination of several of these things will be needed.

In earlier chapters, all the processes you'll follow in making and testing a combination rod have been detailed. Actually, what you're faced with is testing and trying until you hit on the combination of blanks, guides, and grips that will do the job best.

ICE RODS

Making a rod for ice fishing—also called a "jig rod"—can be one of the shortest jobs on record, almost as short as the rod itself. These rods are compact little beauties, designed to do only one job: to bounce a lure on the bottom and lift it up and down in the hope of attracting a cruising fish. The lure is usually a lead-head jig, which in many places goes under the name of "doll fly." Plastic worms or live bait are also used with these short rods.

An ice rod requires no testing of any kind. You need only three items to make one: a short section of an old rod, of solid or tubular fiberglass, or a blank made for this type of rod; a single tiptop; a grip with a chuck and the ferrule that goes with it. How long or how short and how stout you make the ice rod is purely a matter of personal preference. It does need to be sturdy, though. You must lift your fish straight up if you're ice fishing, or horse it up from bottom to boat if you're jigging in Southern waters.

Making the rod is as simple and straightforward as the manner in which it's used. Set the tiptop, fit on the butt ferrule, and you're ready for action. Construction time: 10 minutes, 15 if you add a bit of fancy winding.

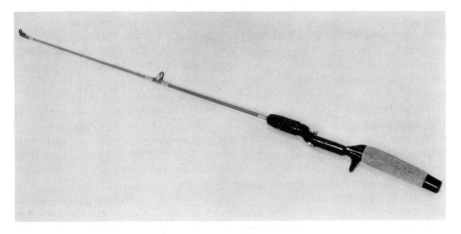

Ice or jig rods generally have blades approximately twice as long as the grip or handle and are fitted with a single ring guide and tiptop.

MUSKIE RODS

In the lakes of the North Central region of the United States and on north into Canada, fishermen who're afflicted with muskie fever equip themselves with special rods before going out to seek the hard-jawed, heavy-bodied muskellunge. Regular baitcast/spincast rods aren't stout enough to handle the oversized plugs or the fish, if they hit one of them—hence the muskie rod.

Muskie rods are a sort of cross between a baitcasting rod and a light boat rod. They're fished with both live bait and lures and have the backbone to set a hook in the muskie's bony jaws. Most muskie rods are 5 to 6 feet long, made on thick-walled fiberglass blanks, and fitted with stainless-steel or tungsten carbide guides. They have a butt grip about one-third longer than those fitted to baitcasting rods, and a foregrip that's 3 or 4 inches long. By tradition as well as because it's needed to handle the fish, muskie rods are equipped with trigger-type reel seats.

On a 6-foot muskie rod, space your guides from the top as follows: 5, 12, 20, 30, and 41 inches. Muskie rod blanks are almost always straight-taper, and this spacing will bring the full backbone into use. You'll want to under-wrap the guides; for a blank this size and heft, a size D or E thread ought to be about right. Incidentally, set the guides on the spine rather than opposite it.

Making a muskie rod involves no drastic changes from any of the procedures given in Chapter 3 and elsewhere. Just remember to build sturdily if you want to hang onto that muskie after you've hooked it.

POPPING RODS

Here we're talking about a cross between a baitcasting rod and a heavy spinning rod. Popping rods are somewhat new to the family of fishing tackle, and there aren't any standards or established traditions to go by.

In fact, popping rods are so new that even skilled rod makers hesitate to define them. I was talking with Bob Hipp, who's in charge of producing Shakespeare's blanks, while gathering data for this book about some of the new trends in tackle. Bob had been telling me about the Shakespeare "bottle blank," which you'll meet on a more formal basis in Chapter 11, and as an afterthought said, "And if you want to trim off the butt section, that Bottle Blank makes a really fine popping rod." Always anxious to get the opinion of experts, I asked, "Bob, how would you define a popping rod?" After a thoughtful pause, he replied, "You know, I was just about to ask you that same question."

We finally agreed that a popping rod can be as light or heavy as a fisherman wants it to be, but no shorter than 6 feet and no longer than 8 feet, and that it should have a fast tip action. And with that definition or description, you'll have to be content.

Light popping rods are sometimes equipped with spinning guides, about as often with ring guides. The choice of guides depends on the reel you plan to use with the rod, and the weight of the rod depends pretty much on your taste. Use a heavy baitcasting or spinning blank, fit a long butt grip and a short foregrip. You can get the spacing for guides—or suggestions as

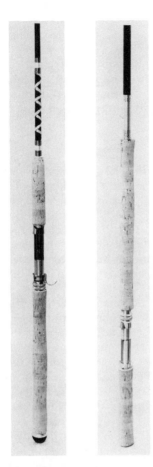

A distinctive mark of the muskie or popping rod (left) is its trigger reel seat. The grip of the two-hand salmon fly rod at right is an elongated and slightly modified Wells.

TEMPLATE PATTERNS FOR GRIPS

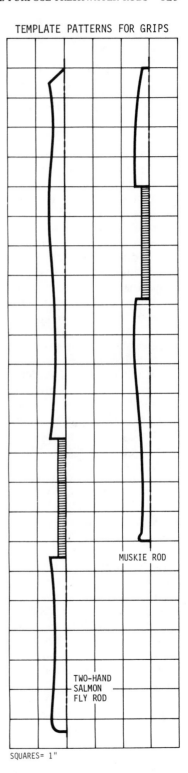

MUSKIE ROD

TWO-HAND
SALMON
FLY ROD

SQUARES= 1"

to where to start testing—from earlier chapters on baitcast/spincast and spinning rods.

Like muskie rods, popping rods are equipped with trigger-type reel seats. That's a tradition, so I was wrong a few paragraphs back when I said popping rods hadn't created any traditions, but this is the only one I know of. Aside from it, the field's wide open and you're limited only by your wishes and ingenuity.

SALMON FLY RODS

We met these long, graceful jobs briefly in the chapter devoted to fly rods but didn't explore building them in any great detail. Unlike popping rods, salmon fly rods have been around a long time and have accumulated enough traditions to share with other kinds of rods. Dedicated fly fishermen like to say that the fly rod is the aristocrat of the fishing tackle world. If this claim is true, then the two-hand salmon fly rod is the aristocrat of the fly rod family. It is the direct descendant of the first recognizable fishing rods, the 16-foot shafts of shaved greenheart and ironwood used in the day of Dame Juliana Berners and Izaak Walton.

In fact, on many English and Scottish estates where the lord of the manor rents rooms and fishing rights to visitors—but keeps title to the fish they catch in his waters—two-hand greenheart and ironwood salmon fly rods are still being used. To an angler unaccustomed to making long casts with a fly rod, the ease with which a caster experienced with the two-hand rod can lay out 125 to 150 feet of line is incredible. The technique of using the two-hand rod is not difficult to master, but in the United States it's really a geographical novelty, its use being confined to the northern portion of the Atlantic seaboard where salmon still run in unpolluted rivers.

With the arrival of graphite, two-hand salmon fly rods are enjoying a revival. Fenwick, Orvis, and Lamiglas list them in their catalogs in lengths of up to 14 feet. The long rod in general appears to be coming back, after the surge in popularity of too-light rods that was begun in the late 1940s by Lee Wulff. Wulff set out to prove two things: that light impregnated bamboo rods, then new, could take big fish in heavy water; and that the hair flies he originated were as effective for salmon as the traditional fly dressings. A very innovative and skilled angler, Wulff was the expert's expert and proved his point. In doing so he caused a lot of anglers to switch to extremely light fly tackle when seeking big fish, and the long two-hand rod went into a partial eclipse.

If you should set out to build a two-hand salmon fly rod, either for fishing or to master the challenge of a new casting skill, you'll find it's really a matter of building an oversized fly rod. These rods require an extremely long grip, between 22 and 24 inches long, with the reel seat beginning 6 to 7 finches from the butt. A hardwood or cork core reel seat with double locking rings for the hood is traditional, as are windings of somewhat restrained character.

Guide spacing is symmetrical and follows the pattern of the spacing given for medium- and slow-action fly rods in Chapter 7. By using the chart there you can work out approximate spacings for two-hand rods of 12 to 14

Specialty Rods

A Ice rod: Plas/Steel blank (solid fiberglass); color, green
Length: 24″ including handle
Weight: Blank, $^5/_{16}$ oz; fitted, 6 oz including handle
Handle: Origin unknown, salvaged from broken rod
Guide: Allan tungsten carbide, tungsten carbide top
Winding: Gudebrod size A; yellow #207

B Muskie or Popping rod: St. Croix blank E15B; color, black
Length: 5½′, 1-piece
Weight: Blank, 2¾ oz; fitted, 8⅝ oz
Grip: Cork, 5″ fore, 12″ butt, rubber butt cap
Reel seat: Allan #51320, chrome-plated brass with trigger
Guides: Fuji Perfection ceramic series; Allan tungsten carbide top
Winding: Gudebrod size E; primary yellow #207; trim green #358

C Travel or Pack rod: Shakespeare blank #120528; color, white
Length: 7′, 4-piece, 24″ breakdown, Sizmatic ferrules
Weight: Blank, 4 oz; fitted, 10¼ oz
Grip: Cork, 4″ fore, 9″ butt, rubber butt cap
Reel seat: Allan #50010
Guides: Allan ceramic CEG series
Winding: Gudebrod size D; primary light blue #230; trim maroon #337

D Two-hand Salmon Fly Rod (#9 or #10 line): Lamiglas blank GFF 1443; color, dark grey
Length: 12′, 3-section, 51″ breakdown, factory ferruled
Weight: Blank, 5¾ oz; fitted, 10$^{15}/_{16}$ oz
Grip: Modified Wells, 12½″ fore, 6½″ butt
Reel seat: Allan #51178, chrome-plated brass
Guides: Fuji BMK ceramic series stripping, #2, #3 and top; BMH ceramic one-foot running
Winding: Gudebrod sizes A & D; primary grey #602 over white #002; trim black/white varigated #8002 at guide stations; size D used on ferrules and at butt

131

feet. The butt guide and the two guides above it should be ceramic insert rings. You'll want to begin with very large snake guides above these three and go down in size to snake guides no smaller than $^1/_0$ at the tip, which should also be of the ceramic insert type. The butt or stripper guide should be set between 20 and 22 inches above the end of the foregrip, the top guide 4 to 5 inches below the tip. In spite of their apparent size, salmon fly rod tips are as delicate as those on other fly rods.

If you're interested enough to make a two-hand salmon fly rod, you'll certainly be interested enough to want to learn the casting technique it requires. Written instructions for doing any kind of casting are not within the scope of this book, but I suggest that you look up the casting club nearest to you—there are such clubs all over the United States now—and ask for the name of a member close to your home. Or, you might consider a brief course at one of the several fishing schools conducted by experts from Orvis, Fenwick, and other tackle makers. Once you've learned to lay out a long line with a two-hand salmon fly rod, you'll have new confidence in your ability to handle regular fly rods.

MAXI-RODS

These are newcomers to freshwater fishing. They were called "bike rods" when they first appeared, the name deriving from the blanks used in making them. These were not rod blanks, but the long, whippy, solid fiberglass staffs attached to trail bikes and dune buggies to carry location flags. These staffs can reach 12 feet in length and are very light and flexible. By splicing two bike rods together, a rod up to 14 feet long can be created suitable for fishing such small baits as single salmon eggs and roe clusters with monofil of 2- to 4-pound test to take very big fish in very fast water.

Dick Swan, the Michigan custom rod maker who fathered these rods, explains their philosophy and physics this way: "The longer the lever (rod) the slower the action and the greater the shock-absorbing qualities it will have. A maxi-rod fights the fish instead of the water; a 3-foot jerk on it will not break a 2-pound-test line. If you have a fish on and can't point the butt of your rod AT your fish with the tip bending beyond the grip by a couple of feet, your rod is too stiff."

Fishermen using maxi-rods in Michigan's steelhead rivers and offshore in the Great Lakes fishing for coho report that it isn't necessary to strike a fish taking a bait when these rods are used. The fish take and move away, setting the hook themselves. Salmon weighing 22 to 23 pounds and steelhead in the 14- to 15-pound class have been taken on 2-pound-test monofil by maxi-rod anglers. As this is being written, the maxi-rod has not yet been widely used, but I see no reason why it shouldn't be effective wherever big, soft-mouthed fish lurk in heavy water.

There are no blanks available commercially on which to make maxi-rods, so you'll have to create your own from scratch. However, Gary Loomis, the manager of Lamiglas's rod and blank manufacturing operations, tells me that the Lamiglas experts are working with Swan in exploring the possibilities of the maxi-rod, so such blanks may be on the market by the time this book reaches you.

Your objective in making a blank for a maxi-rod is to create one that can quite literally be bent into a circle. You might try splicing together a 10-foot bike rod for the butt with a 4-foot soft-action solid fiberglass baitcast/spin-cast blank for a tip. Use the plugging technique illustrated in Chapter 3 in connection with fitting glass-to-glass ferrules, with a section of an old tubular fiberglass rod acting as a sleeve over the joint. Or, you could use two tubular fiberglass soft-action fly or spinning rod blanks and join them with this same method. Since solid fiberglass blades are usually more flexi-ble than tubular ones, experiment with these for tips. It might be necessary to use sections of three blanks to get the extremely soft, whippy action you need and the length you're after, 14 feet or more.

Maxi-rods are usually fitted with straight grips built on the blank in the style of spinning rod grips. Swan says that guide spacing is important. He recommends the use of light stainless-steel or tungsten carbide ring guides, and cautions that the guides must be spaced closely enough so that the line never comes into contact with the rod's surface. This would indicate a spac-ing of 10 to 12 inches from center to center of the guide rings near the butt, and as little as 4- to 6-inch spacing as you approach the tip. As my own suggestion, you might try Gudebrod's Aetna Foulproof guides in this application.

What the maxi-rod really does is to carry us back to the old style of fish-ing, when whippy rods and fragile lines of braided horsehair were the only kind of tackle available. In the short time the maxi-rod has been around, it's established an almost unbelievable record of taking big fish from fast water on the lightest monofil available. If you'd like to meet this kind of challenge, here's your opportunity, in the maxi-rod.

While I'm sure I've missed some types of freshwater rods that are favored in limited geographical areas to meet local conditions, the forego-ing chapters should give you enough scope to make a rod that will match any of these local favorites in performance.

Now, let's go into saltwater.

10

Surf Rods

WITH TUBULAR FIBERGLASS or graphite blanks, surf-fishing enthusiasts can create rods within a few hours. Work on these big blanks moves swiftly. Components such as guides and reel seats are large; threads are heavy, which makes winding easy and fast; guide spacing is straightforward. Unless you favor cork grips, preformed foam plastic grips can be fitted to save time waiting for glued-up cork grips to dry. You can quite literally make up a rod in the early evening hours and be using it on your favorite stretch of beach by daylight or tide change the next morning.

You can design your surfcasting rod to be used with either a conventional revolving spool reel or a surf spinning reel; the difference is merely one of guide selection. You must decide on one or the other, though, for the large ring guides required to control heavy monofil call for butt guides that are incompatible with a revolving spool reel.

Among the things you can do quite readily is designing your surf rod to have the action, weight, length, grip or handle diameter, and other features that suit you precisely. You can tailor your blank to provide fast tip or slower action, and can put together a rod that will handle terminal tackle that differs in weight of sinker and bait by as much as 5 or 6 ounces.

Surf rod blanks can stand a lot more adjusting in their making than can the more delicate and demanding blanks on which freshwater rods are built. For instance, a 9-foot blank can be extended by as much as 12 to 18 inches by inserting a dowel—made from the butt of an old pool cue, if you can find one—to create faster tip action. Cutting 5 to 8 inches from the tip results in a slower action. If you want to build an unusually light rod, the butt grip can be fitted in two pieces, leaving the blade exposed between them. If you prefer a hefty rod, you can always stay with the traditional wooden handle fitted with a ferrule to the blank. This will extend the blank's length by a couple of feet and give you a substantially faster tip, so if you do use this kind of handle you might want to trim the tip a few inches.

Basically, surf spinning rods are scaled-up versions of their freshwater cousins, just as surfcasting rods designed for use with wooden handles are magnified baitcasting rods. Fishermen who do a lot of surfcasting generally favor fast-tip rods if they're using spinning reels; users of revolving spool reels usually want a more deliberate timing in their rods. I've already mentioned two ways you can use to alter the action of a blank without harming its performance. The action of an altered rod will be different, of course, but the overall performance in terms of casting distance or weight of terminal tackle you can use or the rod's ability to handle a fish will be only minimally affected.

By now most anglers realize that surfcasters and saltwater fishermen generally, for that matter, don't use big gear because they expect to catch big fish. In the late 1940s, when the virtues of light tackle were being widely debated and discussed, Jason Lucas, one of the leading anglers and outdoor writers of the time, landed several saltwater fish weighing between 12 and 20 pounds using a light baitcasting rod and ordinary sewing thread. It took him an hour or more to tire each of his catches before they could be brought to gaff, but Lucas proved a point that novice saltwater anglers often overlook: it's not the line test or the power of a rod that brings in a fish, but the fisherman's ability to play it until it can be safely landed.

This certainly isn't a recommendation that you begin using a baitcasting rod and sewing thread for surf fishing. Lucas was an extraordinarily skillful angler, and his stunt was just that, a stunt to prove a point.

ROD DESIGN

No one knows better than you do the kind of surf rod that fits your need. You'll know whether you want a short rod that will hit the holes close in, or a long one that will flip 5 ounces of lead and a couple of ounces of bait out where the waves break or where there's an underwater reef. I'm not going to suggest the type or kind of rod you want to make, but will remind you of a few things you may overlook if you're an old surf fisherman but a new rod maker.

There's a great deal of difference between fiberglass and graphite blanks in addition to their cost. To those accustomed to handling heavy tackle, the weight difference is at first unbelievable. In blanks of equal length, a graphite blank will weigh just a bit more than half as much as a thick-wall fiberglass blank and about one-third as much as a thin-wall fiberglass blank. During a day of casting, that's a lot of difference. The only exception to this is Fenwick's Feralite, a high-density thin-wall fiberglass that weighs only about one-third more than a graphite blank in rods of equal length and action.

When you design your surf rod, don't fall in love with the idea of a center ferrule. Yes, it's nice to have sections of equal length, but often center-ferruling will not bring out the best in a rod's action. This is especially true of heavy-duty rods, which must have sturdy ferrules. Check the blank before you make your final decision on its design. You can do this in either of two ways. One way is to attach a weight representing the total of your usual cast, lead plus bait, to the tip of the blank and then raise the butt until it's at about a 35° to 45° angle to the floor. Make a mental note where the blank begins to straighten out of its arc toward the butt. If you're after maximum tip action, put your ferrule at that point. Incidentally, if you're testing a graphite blank, be careful not to raise the butt at an angle greater than 30° to 35°. The danger of imposing a constant static load on graphite blanks has been noted earlier.

An alternative method of determining the power axis of a heavy-duty blank—and again, this isn't recommended for graphite—is to hold the blank parallel to the ground while you stand in front of a wall with the butt in your hand. (Before starting, protect the tip of the blank with several turns of masking tape.) Press the tip of the blank against the wall and push the butt forward slowly and steadily. As in the previous method of testing with a static weight, the point at which the tip straightens out of its arc will be the power axis and consequently the spot at which to set the center ferrule.

Before installing the ferrule, plug both ends of the butt section and the bottom end of the upper section. Many tackle dealers who stock make-it-yourself lure items carry basswood blanks from which casting lures are made, and these blanks make excellent plugs, being light in weight and of wood that's easy to work. Be sure to taper the tops of the plugs so there will be no hard edge to press against a flexed rod wall. Set the plugs with an elastic adhesive rather then epoxy, which sets up brittle.

Most surf rods require a reel seat with an ID of at least $7/_8$ inch, and you may be at a loss for bushings of such a large size. If there's a supply source for ready-made bushings, I haven't found it yet, and for a while made them from sheet cork, which is much more fragile than specie cork such as that used in grip rings. In many cases, I found that a single turn of cork sheet would form a bushing, resulting in so little material between the reel seat and the blank that the possibility of the seat biting into the fiberglass was a source of concern.

Finally, a rod-making friend—I've forgotten who—advised me to use ordinary package sealing tape, not the kind with pressure-sensitive adhesive, but the old-fashioned glue-coated variety. The tape stuck to itself well enough, but didn't adhere to the rod. A dab of shellac solved that problem, though any rod-making adhesive would probably work as well.

To form these bushings, wrap the tape on the rod after wetting the stickum side thoroughly, enough to make the paper limp. Wrap in straight courses, not in a spiral, using two or three courses, as shown in the pictures. Avoid wrinkles and creases. When the tape has dried overnight, it will slip off the tapered blank; be sure to mark the points at which it will be replaced. Brush these areas with shellac and let it get tacky, then slide the roll back on the blank. Next, give the edges of each course of tape and their outer surfaces a thin shellac coating as a protection against moisture. If you make the bushings a bit oversized and sand them for a snug reel-seat fit, do the sanding before applying the shellac. Use your regular adhesive to set the reel seat.

Having had a few unhappy experiences with early aluminum reel seats on saltwater rods, my prejudice against aluminum fittings on these rods leads me to recommend chrome- or nickel-plated reel seats for them. The double-ring variety is pretty much standard on such reel seats, and that extra locking ring is very low-cost insurance.

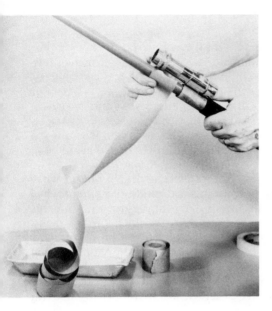

Plain brown paper parcel-sealing tape 1½ to 2 inches wide makes very sturdy reel-seat bushings for heavy-duty rods such as this surf spinning rod. Use the old-fashioned mucilage-coated tape, not the kind with self-sticking adhesive. First, measure the amount required to build up to the required diameter to fit the reel seat.

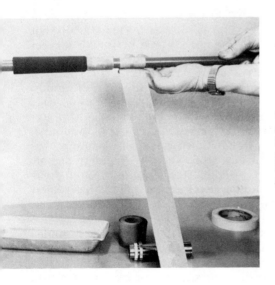

Wet the tape—an ice-cube tray makes a good water pan—and form the bushing on the blank. When completely dry, the bushing will slip off the blank; it is then brushed with shellac and set with adhesive.

GUIDES

In Chapter 6, there's a chart giving suggested guide spacings for heavy spinning rods, while a similar chart in Chapter 5 gives spacings for heavy-duty baitcasting rods. If you're making a surf spinning rod, you'll find the suggestions usable for rods of up to 10 feet; for longer rods you'll probably need to adjust them, and perhaps add one more guide for surf spinning rods in the 12-foot plus range. But at the risk of being repetitious, I must stress again that guide settings should be determined by testing if you want optimum performance.

Test methods outlined in Chapters 5 and 6 can be used to check guide settings on saltwater as well as freshwater rods. You're looking for the same sources of problems, and the basic methods of curing them are the same regardless of the weight and length of the blank.

While the heavy monofil used in saltwater angling isn't as subject to the tendency to sag and cling to the rod's surface that characterizes lightweight monofil, you want a rod on which you can use light-test mono if you wish, without the danger of line cling and slap. The tests will help you avoid both problems.

Your final test should be of the butt guide's placement. No matter what spacing charts suggest, this test is to spinning rod guide placement what acid is to a metals assayer. To summarize it briefly: fit the rod with the reel you plan to use and with monofil of the weight with which you normally fish. Pass the monofil through all the guides and anchor it at the tip with masking tape, then wind the reel just enough to bring the monofil taut, without strain. The line should then be perfectly straight from the reel to the center of the second guide and should just touch the top of the arc made by the ring of the butt guide. The picture shows you exactly what to look for.

You should make the same test with a surfcasting rod that will be fitted with ring guides for use with a revolving-spool reel. To get consistently long, free-flowing casts, placement of the butt guide is extremely important.

Guide selection and guide size are equally important. On a surf spinning rod which you plan to use with 14- to 20-pound monofil, your butt guide should be no smaller than 60mm, and if you habitually use mono in tests above 20 pounds, go to a 70mm butt guide. Don't try to choke down too quickly the spiral made by the monofil as it leaves the reel spool by a quick reduction of guide diameters. You can step down as much as 10mm, sometimes as much as 12mm, between the butt guide and the second guide, but if your line-flow test indicates that you should step down only 8mm, don't hesitate to use the larger sized second guide. Once the monofil has passed through the three guides at the bottom of the rod, it loses its tendency to belly, and you can step down guide diameters much more rapidly.

Heavy monofil naturally creates more drag as it goes through guides than does the lighter test mono used in freshwater fishing, so chrome-plated stainless-steel guides are about your best bet, since ceramic insert guides aren't available in the large diameters called for by surf spinning rods. The largest diameter insert guides with which I'm familiar are 30mm, so your best bets are chrome-plated stainless steel, tungsten carbide, or hard stainless steel, and these are all available in ring sizes up to 70mm. You can and should fit your surf spinning rod with a ceramic insert tiptop, however, for heavy monofil scores guides quite seriously.

I must repeat here the recommendation I made earlier about not undersizing the guides on a surfcasting rod that's going to be used with a revolving-spool reel. Some surfcasting reels are quite wide, and you can look for 3 to 5 inches of lateral line play as the line peels off. A 20mm butt guide, stepping down to 14, 12, and 10mm, will improve your casting by reducing line friction. Insert guides are available in all the sizes you'll normally require, as are tungsten carbide, gold-plated tungsten carbide, and hard stainless-steel guides.

GRIPS

Surfcasting rods can be fitted with several kinds of grips, and the traditional butt grip, middle grip, and foregrip can also be replaced by a single wound-on grip of medium-sized cotton cordage running from the butt to above the reel. I specify cotton, because nylon and other synthetics can be very rough on the hands as well as being slick when wet. Cork grips on surfcasting rods are gradually giving way to synthetic foam grips. The best-known of these are made by Featherweight and sold under their trademarked names of Foamlite and Hypalon. Foamlite is available in lengths from 3 to 13 inches, and inside diameters up to $^{15}/_{16}$ inch; Hypalon comes in 5- to 13-inch lengths, and the largest inside diameter available in this material is $^{7}/_{8}$ inch. These preformed grips simply slip down on the rod and are cemented in place.

Of the two, Foamlite is much more flexible and easier to fit. Factory installations are made by shooting a blast of compressed air into the top of the grip and pulling it down as it rides on the air cushion thus created. Chances are, though, that you'll be fitting a grip of this type by hand, and you'll appreciate the greater flexibility of Foamlite. The best way I've found to handle Foamlite grips is to push them down from their top ends until a bulge is created, then quickly pull the bottom of the grip down, stretching out the bulge. Hypalon, because of its greater stiffness, must be twisted back and forth while pulling from the bottom.

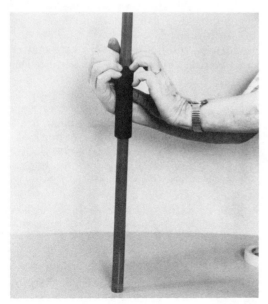

This is the easiest way to slide a Foamlite grip on a rod. Push down with your fingertips from the top, stopping every foot or so to pull the bottom of the grip along. Coating the blank with adhesive or soap helps. If you use soap, you can trickle adhesive between blank and grip after the grip is placed.

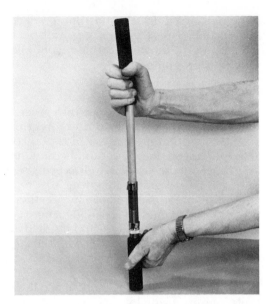

Hypalon grips, stiffer and less flexible than their Foamlite cousins, must be pulled on a blank with a rotary motion, with your hands at the bottom of the grip. Soap or adhesive also helps in sliding Hypalon grips into position.

Coating the blank with soapsuds helps to slide these grips in place. When you reach a point about 3 inches above the top of the spot where the grip will be seated, wipe the blank dry and switch to plain water as a lubricant, or coat the blank with a slow-setting liquid adhesive for the final few inches above the top seating line. Wipe off excess adhesive after the grip is in place, using the solvent recommended by its maker. If you fit the grips without using any kind of lubricant, you can glue them later by pulling the rims away from the blank and trickling a few drops of adhesive into the gap. These grips have a high coefficient of skin friction, and you don't need much adhesive to hold them firmly in place.

Fitting a wooden handle on a surfcasting rod is a straightforward matter of seating the blank in a locking butt ferrule that is part of the handle. Details are given in a later chapter.

In common with all saltwater rods, surf rods should be double-wrapped. Use a size E or EE thread, and when the winding job is finished, apply a double or triple layer of epoxy coating over the windings, or you can use a good varnish. Both these coatings are easier to handle and give better looking results if you apply two or three thin coats rather than trying to do the job with a single heavy coating. Be sure the undercoats are bone-dry before adding the second and third. I've never tried using an infrared lamp to speed up the drying of rod coatings. Someone may have done so, but I've been afraid the light's rays might do some hidden damage to the fiberglass or graphite of the blank. Infrared is concentrated sunshine, and the sun is one of the chief causes of rod deterioration.

Surf fishing is one of angling's most challenging forms, with its long casts and the extensive time often required to bring in hooked fish. You'll enjoy it even more than you do now when you head for your favorite strip of beach or rocky shoreline carrying a rod you've made yourself.

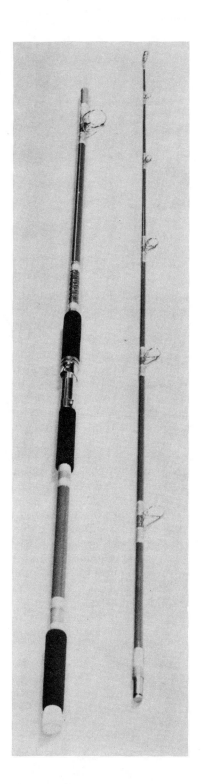

Surf Spinning Rod

St. Croix blank #12SU; color, tan
Length: 10′, 2-piece, 60″ breakdown, Sizmatic
ferrule
Weight: Blank, 9¾ oz; fitted, 16 $^{15}/_{16}$ oz
Grip: Foamlite 6″ butt, center and fore
Reel seat: Allan #51012, chrome-plated brass
Guides: Allan VSPG series, chromed stainless
steel
Winding: Gudebrod size E; primary fluorescent
yellow; trim fluorescent green

11

Boat/Pier Rods

THIS MAY WELL be the most diversified of all fishing rod families, and the one with the most complicated—even confused—number of names. When we say "fly" or "baitcasting" or "spinning" rod, we get a pretty specific mental picture of what we're talking about. When we say "boat" or "pier" or "jetty" or, as I've written at the head of the chapter, "boat/pier rod," the picture tends to blur a bit. Perhaps this is because no other type of rod has so many different names and appears in such varied versions. The boat/pier or jetty rod is also called a "bay rod," a "shore rod," a "jig rod," a "cod rod," and I'm sure there are other names that have escaped me for this type of rod, which by any of its names is basically the same piece of tackle.

To avoid confusing things, we're going to call them all "boat/pier" rods in this chapter, whether the rod is equipped with a roller top for light trolling as well as bait fishing, or whether it's wrapped heavily in its center section and called a "cod rod."

What we're talking about is a group of rods that can be anywhere from 4 to 8 feet long, with actions a bit on the stiff side, that can be fitted optionally with wooden handles, chuck-type grips, or integral cork or foam plastic grips. Rods in this family can be fitted with small-diameter spinning guides, ring guides, or light roller guides, or a combination of ring guides and roller guides and tops. In this last version, the practice is to set a roller butt or lead guide and then two or three ring guides and a roller tiptop. As you've gathered by now, boat/pier rods are saltwater workhorses, a sort of all-purpose category, with many versions. The use to which you put such a rod should guide you in selecting the proper blank and fittings.

BLANK TYPES

If most of your fishing is done from a pier or jetty, or if you take your own tackle out on party boats, then you'll want a blank that's in the 4- to 6-foot range, with fairly stiff tip action. The blank can be either solid or tubular fiberglass or graphite. This kind of fishing doesn't require long casts, and when you're shoulder-to-shoulder with other anglers on a pier or party boat, the emphasis is not on playing your fish, but on bringing them in quickly to avoid fouling the lines of others. Rods of this kind are usually fitted with a wooden handle and conventional ring guides.

On the other hand, if most of your fishing is drifting live bait from a skiff, or fishing close inshore from the bank in areas where the long casts of a surf rod aren't necessary to reach productive spots, you'll want a longer blank with a more sensitive tip. If you use your boat/pier rod for light trolling, especially with a metal line, you may forego the lighter tip and fit the blank with a roller tiptop and butt guide. There are a number of blanks that allow you to choose any of these options when making them into a rod.

Perhaps the most versatile, and certainly the one easiest and most economical to fit, is Shakespeare's "bottle blank," which got its name for reasons that the accompanying picture makes obvious. The blank is 6 feet 8 inches long and weighs 13 ounces raw, and is remarkably easy to fit. The bottom bulge accepts a $^7/_8$-inch butt cap and serves as a handle without any additions or alterations, while the second bulge accepts $^5/_8$- to $^7/_8$-inch ID reel seats with a minimum of bushing, and is long enough to be fitted with a foam or cork foregrip. The tip can be shortened if you're planning a light trolling rod, or a pier rod, or left as is for boat fishing with live bait. A trigger reel seat turns the blank into a popping rod.

Rawhide's SW80 and SW90 series of blanks give you about the same degree of versatility. These blanks range in length from 8 to 9 feet and are very adaptable to such alterations as extending their length by splicing on a butt extension—in the form of a pool cue or study hardwood dowel—or they can be shortened by trimming butts or tips to make them suitable for pier or trolling use.

There's a wide variety of blanks available from other makers. These range from $4^1/_2$- to 5- and 6-foot jobs that can be fitted with wooden handles

One of the easiest heavy-duty blanks to turn into a finished rod is Shakespeare's "bottle blank," with its preformed foregrip/reel seat and handle. This is the blank before fitting.

This is the bottle blank after it has been fitted with reel seat, short foregrip, guides, and windings. This version is designed as a boat/pier rod, with tungsten carbide Allan guides.

to produce rods 6 to 8 feet long, having almost any range of actions you might fancy. You know your own requirements better than anyone else, and it's up to you to scan the catalogs and pick out the blank that appeals to you the most. What we're going to do here is not to select blanks, but to look at the common denominators involved in turning the blank into a rod.

FITTING PROCEDURES

Locating the spine on a heavy saltwater blank can sometimes be done by simple observation. If the blank has a clear or translucent finish, you may be able to detect the minute irregularities that mark the joining of the outside wrapping. On heavy-duty blanks, with their big diameters, this joining can be seen more readily than it can on light blanks that have a finer meshed outside covering. If the blank has been enameled, as are a number of saltwater jobs, you can sand off the bottom enamel for an inch or so from the butt, where the handle ferrule will hide it, and find the spine line. Solid glass blanks, of course, have no spines, but are uniform in action in all areas of their circumference.

All the steps in fitting a saltwater rod are the same as those detailed in Chapter 3 for fitting freshwater blanks; the difference is chiefly one of size. The procedures are followed in the same order: ferrules, grips, guides, winding. Some construction details are of greater importance on saltwater blanks than on the lighter blanks that make up into freshwater rods. One of these is plugging the blanks at their butts and center-ferruling points. Saltwater tackle must be prepared to accept stresses not commonly encountered by that used in freshwater fishing.

Take the matter of ferruling, for instance. Most of the better saltwater anglers I know prefer to leave the blades of their rods in one piece and fit them with handles equipped with butt ferrules. This is almost a must in heavy trolling rods, which we'll meet in the next chapter, but isn't really all that necessary in blanks designed for less strenuous service as boat/pier rods. Center-ferruling these rods makes them a lot easier to carry from place to place in a car, or on a plane.

You can, as already noted, add an integral handle to a boat/pier rod by using an old pool cue—often hard to find—or a piece of $3/4$- or 1-inch ash dowel, which is almost equally strong. Taper the end of the dowel to match the inside taper of the blank. You do this by starting at the tip of the dowel and working the taper with a file until the first inch or so of the dowel slips into the bottom of the blank. Keep working down on the dowel, an inch or so at a time, testing often. Don't force the dowel into the butt, but keep removing material and testing for fit by inserting the tapered end and revolving it slowly inside the blank. This will show high spots on the dowel or on the inner wall of the blank, which can be seen in places rubbed by the contact between plug and wall.

Six to eight inches is about the minimum amount of taper that's safe to work. Anything under 6 inches might not be enough splice area, depending on the weight of the blank and its wall thickness. You can get by with shorter plugs on thick-wall blanks. Set the tapered extension into the butt of the blank with epoxy. If you begin with a length of cue stick or dowel that's longer than the completed extension will be, you can then trim the extension to size and ferrule the blank at its center.

Sand the extension glass-smooth before you try to put on a foam grip; these have already been discussed in Chapter 10, along with the way to fit them. If you plan your extension so that the splice falls under the reel seat, you'll have a virtual guarantee that the butt of your rod won't give way even under the most severe stress.

There's a way to build up your own handle for a light boat/pier rod that is quick and easy. You'll need a length of thin-wall aluminum electrical conduit, with a $^1/_2$-inch OD, as long as the handle plus the butt cap; a piece of $^3/_8$-inch dowel; a ferrule that fits the butt of the blank—usually this will be about 32/64 to 36/64; and foam butt and foregrips—a good combination is a 4- or 5-inch foregrip and a 7- to 12-inch butt grip.

A $^3/_8$-inch dowel fits snugly inside a length of $^1/_2$-inch thin-wall conduit; you may have to do a bit of light sanding to remove high spots or to allow the dowel to accommodate small internal irregularities in the conduit. Reduce one end of the dowel with file and sandpaper to fit the female ferrule. Refer to Chapter 3 for hints on measuring and cutting for ferrule in-

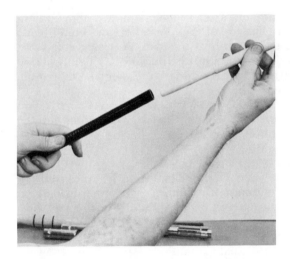

The butt ends of most saltwater blanks, such as this one by Rawhide, are almost straight cylinders, which makes it simple to form plugs with no tool other than a file.

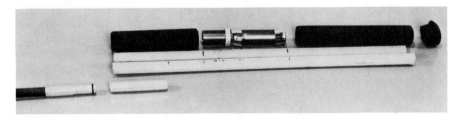

Components for a butt-ferruled saltwater boat rod handle are the ferrule, left; a length of ⅜-inch ash dowel, bottom center; a length of ½-inch OD aluminum electrical conduit; Foamlite or Hypalon grips, and reel seat.

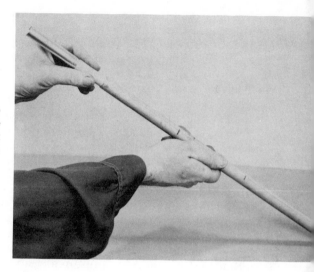

After fitting the female ferrule to one end of the dowel, coat the dowel with epoxy and slide it into the conduit. It will be a tight, push fit.

stallation. Ferrules in the outside-diameter range mentioned above will fit snugly inside $1/2$-inch conduit. The top of the female ferrule should be no more than $1/16$ to $1/8$ inch above the top of the conduit. Using epoxy, set the ferrule on the dowel and the dowel inside the conduit. The resulting handle, when reel seat and grips have been added, will weigh no more than a comparable wooden handle.

One of the advantages of detachable handles on saltwater rods is that you can switch blades in them to suit your wishes or needs. The strength of the handle-blade combination resulting from the foregoing job is adequate for anything except heavy-duty trolling.

For any boat/pier rod's reel seat, I'll still choose chrome- or nickel-plated brass over aluminum. Granted that modern anodizing has removed the curse of saltwater corrosion of aluminum rod fittings, my unhappy past experiences with the action of saltwater on exposed nonferrous metals leave my prejudice intact. Aluminum must be washed in fresh water after a day's fishing, and this is often forgotten or is inconvenient to do. Plated metals don't require this kind of immediate attention. Apparently a lot of

After setting the reel seat on a paper or string bushing, slide on the grips and attach a butt cap to the handle; then fit the male ferrule to the butt of the blank. Overall length of the handle shown above is 20 inches, and the rod blade is 50 inches.

Boat/Pier Rods

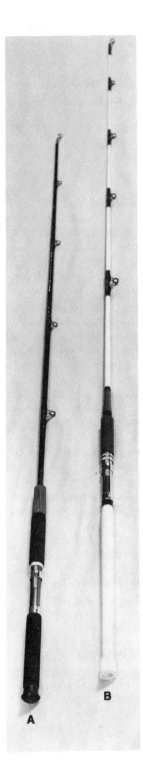

A **Light:** Plas/Steel blank (solid fiberglass); color, black
Length: 4½', 1-piece blade butt-ferruled with Sizmatic to fit handle
Weight: Blank, 5⅞ oz; fitted, 9¼ oz
Handle: Hypalon fore and butt, Glad short fore on blade; butt grips over aluminum wood-cored, rubber butt cap
Reel seat: Allan #50010
Guides: Allan tungsten carbide, tungsten carbide top
Winding: Gudebrod size E; primary black #001 double-wound; trim black/yellow varigated #8209

B **Medium:** Shakespeare blank #120019 ('bottle blanl'); color, white
Length: 6' 8", 1-piece
Weight: Blank, 10½ oz; fitted, 16^{15}/$_{16}$ oz
Handle: Integral with blank; 4" foregrip, neoprene foam filled industrial hose, green
Reel seat: Allan #51178, chrome-plated brass
Guides: Allan tungsten carbide, tungsten carbide top
Winding: Gudebrod size E; primary dark green #5896 double-wound; trim light green #358

saltwater anglers feel as I do about this, for I see very few aluminum fittings on saltwater rods.

You have a lot of options in selecting guides for a boat/pier rod. Braced guides are a must, for the guides on a heavy-duty rod take a lot of stresses. Stainless steel, either hardened or chrome-plated, is a good choice. So are ceramic insert guides, which have heavily plated metal parts; these are less likely to be scored by big monofil lines than are steel guides. Tungsten carbide (also known by the trade name Carboloy) guides are almost as score-resistant as ceramic or aluminum oxide insert guides. On rods that will be used with wire lines, roller guides are a must, with tungsten carbide a second choice.

Guide spacing is quite straightforward on boat/pier rods. You will find that most of these blanks are designed with straight tapers, and can safely use the chart given in Chapter 5 for approximate spacing of guides on straight-taper baitcasting rods. This will at least get you started; but saltwater blanks are as individualistic as their freshwater cousins, and you must still arrive at a final spacing after you've tested your initial efforts, using the procedures given in detail in earlier chapters.

Double-winding, or under-wrapping as it's sometimes called, is a very good idea on saltwater rods. When you double-wrap, you should mark spacings from the center ring of each guide before you put on the first winding. The pictures give the details of how to go about this. Once you've established the spacing for the first winding, it's easy to judge by eye where you begin your winding over the guide feet. If you're using a light and a dark color in your double-winding, the light color should always be under the dark color; dark colors may bleed through lighter overwindings. You can minimize the danger of this happening by using Gudebrod's NCP—No Color Preservative—threads for your windings.

Boat/pier rods are husky enough in the butt to carry almost any kind of decorative winding you might care to apply, so let your creative instincts run wild when you apply the finishing touches. And remember, when it comes to adding the varnish or epoxy, two thin coats are better than one thick coat; three thin coats are better than two medium-thick ones. An extra coat is a very small amount of insurance to carry on a rod that you've worked hard in making.

Let me close this chapter with a short observation based on years of building and using rods of all types. Saltwater or fresh, there's really no such thing as a multipurpose rod, one that will give real pleasure and total satisfaction in each mode of use. If you divide your offshore angling almost equally between stillfishing from a pier or jetty and trolling without a downrigger, you need separate rods for these two methods. If you use a downrigger or do most of your fishing from a boat, you'll get more sport and more enjoyment when using rods made for these types of angling.

It's really just that simple. By making your own rods, you can afford specialized tackle of the different kinds that add pleasure to your hours on the water.

12

Regulation Tackle Rods

THESE ARE THE real huskies of the rod family, built like the middle linebackers of a pro football team. If you're trolling offshore in search of a fish that will win recognition as a record-breaker, the odds are ten to one that you'll be using a regulation tackle rod.

What the phrase actually means is that the rod is tailored to handle line of a specific breaking test, ranging from 20 to 180 pounds. Thus, regulation tackle rods are described as "20-pound," "30-pound," "50-pound," "80-pound," "130-pound," and "180-pound" rods. If you take a fish on a 30-pound RT rod using 40-pound test line, your catch will not be recognized as a record within that class; it must be judged in the "unlimited" category—tackle meeting no precise specifications—in which weight records are often awesome. Record-breaking fish in this category may have been caught with a rod far in excess of regulation size, using line testing at 200 pounds or more.

Who says this must be the case? The International Game Fish Association, abbreviated as IGFA, which is the quasi-official international group given the job of judging and certifying record-breaking catches. Oddly enough, the IGFA's own rules have little to say about rods. The rules go into very precise and minute detail regarding the lines used, how they are tested for breaking strain, how they must be rigged, and so on. All that the rules say about rods, however, is that they "must be in accordance with sporting ethics and customs." The rest is silence.

Now, this doesn't mean that you must all by yourself engineer a rod that will meet these vague specifications. Tackle manufacturers do this for you; they tailor blanks that are accepted by IGFA in all the six categories. But if you take a record-breaking fish on a rod-line combination that is mismatched according to IGFA standards—that is, a line lighter or heavier than the designated test of the rod—it's back to square one and into the "unlimited" classification for your prize catch. Mismatching rod and line is not considered by IGFA to be "in accordance with sporting ethics."

Actually, the six "designated" categories have effectively been reduced to five in recent years by another IGFA ruling. A fish taken on 180-pound test tackle is now recognized as a world's record only if it exceeds the weight of a fish of the same species already recognized as holding an "unlimited" class record. If this seems to you to be arbitrary and an effort to preserve a questionable status quo, you're not alone. However, the circle of anglers who devote their time, energy, and considerable amounts of money to seeking record-breaking catches is a small and pretty well closed one, so all that the fishermen outside it can do is accept things as they are.

If you want to join the record-breaker club, though, you'll adhere to IGFA standards and hope that lightning will strike in the form of a big fish, while you're using a "regulation tackle" rod and a line of the correct weight. Be confident that the blank you buy on which to make an RT rod will meet IGFA approval, regardless of who makes it, or where. Your real decision is what kind of saltwater fish you're going to try for. If it's marlin or tuna, you'll be looking for a blank in the 130-pound category; if it's amberjack or sailfish, the blank will be in the 30-pound or 20-pound class.

Typical saltwater handles: (**A**) traditional varnished ash by Allan; (**B**) AFTCO's aluminum and black anodized aluminum handles; (**C**) fiberglass-cored handle by Sabre, with offset aluminum reel seat; (**D**) varnished ash light-duty handle by Varmac.

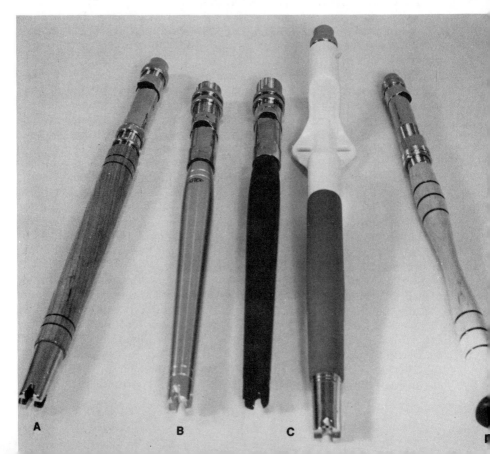

A   B   C

FITTING PROCEDURES

Just as specifications for competition or RT rod blanks have become standardized, so have the fittings. Your RT rod will be fitted with roller guides, and the guides will be double- or triple-wound, with preference leaning toward the latter. It will be fitted into a detachable handle having a double-locking reel seat. Today, the handle is as likely to be aluminum, stainless steel, or a foam-covered shaft of heavy, solid fiberglass fitted with a plated reel seat and gimbal as it is to be made of the traditional varnished ash or hickory. The photo shows types of handles commonly fitted to RT rods, though the style of bent handle favored by some saltwater anglers is not included. However, the illustration does show one of the offset reel-seat handles that's becoming increasingly popular because of the more direct line path they give from reel to guides.

Your major job in converting a blank into an RT rod is going to be shaping a bushing or butt plug, and often the two can be combined. However, if the OD of the blank is more than $1/32$ inch smaller than the ID of the butt ferrule, make bushing and plug separately. This isn't a major job, even without a lathe. RT butt ferrules come in diameters of .810, .960, or 1.200 inch, so ferrule plugs can be formed from $5/8$-, $3/4$-, or 1-inch ash dowel stock with very little filing and sanding. Your objective is a snug but not a push fit; you should leave enough room for a good dollop of epoxy—the best adhesive for this particular job.

Use cotton twine for a bushing, or you can use the type of paper bushing described in an earlier chapter. Twine or paper should both be coated with shellac and allowed to dry thoroughly before being set into the ferrule. The pictures give details of bushing making.

Remember when you make your plug to allow for the cross-brace that's in the bottom of locking reel-seat or butt ferrules. This is not merely a brace to give the assembly added strength, but a means of aligning the blade with the reel seat. Before gluing up the bushing assembly, be sure the blank's spine is in alignment with the reel seat as well as with the vee that must be filed in the base of the bushing to secure the proper guide alignment.

Guide spacing on RT rods is symmetrical and is basically the same as that given in the chart in Chapter 5, which suggests approximate spacing for 5-foot baitcasting rods with straight-taper walls. But remember that saltwater reels are big fellows, and check out the butt guide in its relationship to the reel to make sure you've got a true and free line path. Finally, fit the foregrip on the rod butt.

On light RT blanks, those in the 20-pound or 30-pound class, double-winding is a must, and even on these peewees of the RT family, triple-winding is a good idea. This is especially true if you're using straddle guides of the Mildrum type.

After you've determined the guide spacing, mark the center line of each guide and mark also the point at which its feet end, plus about 1 inch. Wind the first course from end to end, using EE or E thread. Be sure to mark the center on the underwrapping. Then, wind on the guide with the second wrapping, in a contrasting or complementary color of thread, carrying the

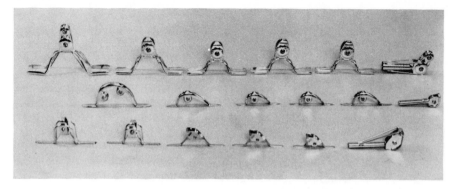

Roller guides for saltwater trolling rods. Top: Mildrum's straddle-foot guides and tiptop; AFTCO's hard-chromed guides and tiptop; bottom: Allan's Oilite self-lubricating guides and tiptop.

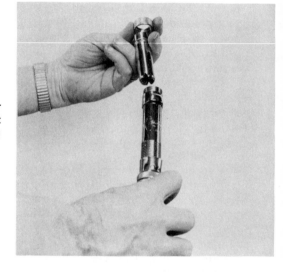

Components of a typical saltwater handle: from top, locking ring, butt ferrule, reel seat with double-locking rings at bottom.

Butt ferrules of saltwater trolling rods require a bushing, as they are usually anywhere from ⅛ to 1½ inches larger in inside diameter than the outside diameter of the blank's butt. To make a combination bushing and plug from a piece of ash dowel, mark the depth of the ferrule and the length of the plug on the dowel, then form the bushing-plug with file and sandpaper as already detailed.

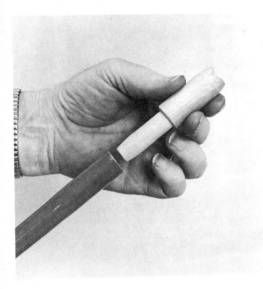

Be sure to taper the top half-inch of the plug so it won't form a sharply defined contact line inside the blank. Set the plug with epoxy and let dry before fitting the ferrule. Be sure the notched butt of the ferrule is aligned with the blank's spine so that the plane of spine and reel seat coincide.

winding to within about $^{1}/_{4}$ inch of the end of the underwrap. Finally, add the third course of thread, making it another $^{1}/_{4}$ inch shorter than the second course. The exposed ends of the varicolored threads provide all the decorative touches the rod needs.

Epoxy coating is better than varnish for saltwater rods. When you varnish a winding that contains several layers of thread, allow plenty of liquid and plenty of time for it to soak through to the bottom layer. You must be ready to daub on extra liquid as it soaks into the winding. Be sure all the tiny gaps between the threads of the winding are filled with the first coat. Brush the epoxy on first by rotating the rod, then smooth the coat with

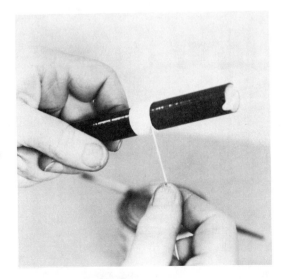

When fitting a blank with a butt only fractionally smaller than the ID of the ferrule, make a bushing from cotton twine. Wind the twine on the butt just as you'd wind threads on a blank.

Test the bushing for size—the ferrule should slip on easily, without force being required.

Saturate the twine with shellac and let dry thoroughly; this makes the twine almost as hard as metal and attaches it firmly to the blank. Set the ferrule with epoxy. The twine corrugations give plenty of "tooth" between blank and ferrule for excellent adhesion.

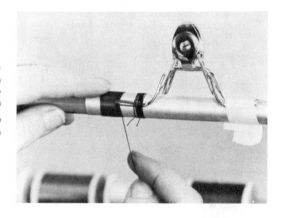

Always set saltwater rod guides on an underwrap, especially Mildrum-type straddle-foot guides. A better, tighter winding on the feet will be obtained if you make a temporary winding at the start of the braces to keep feet in close contact with the blank.

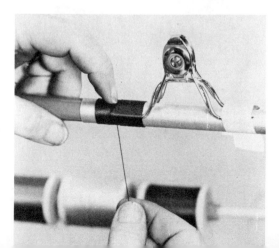

Double-wrapping is the rule on heavy-duty saltwater trolling rods, and triple-winding is often used. To double-wind, carry the first course of thread over the guide feet to the braces, then reverse and over-wind back to within about ⅛ inch of the toes. Pull under with a loop as usual. To triple-wind, after pulling the double-wound thread under, start a course of a different color thread on top of it and carry the winding over the feet to the braces.

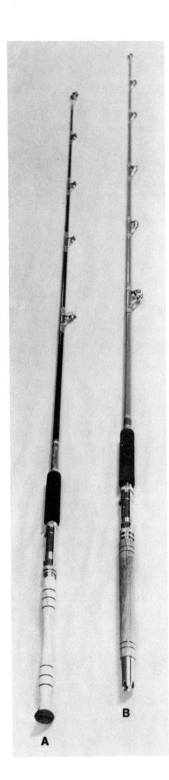

RT Rods

A **20#:** Rawhide blank #SW8040; color, maroon
Length: 5' 10", tip shortened from original length
Weight: Blank, 6⅞ oz; fitted, 10 ¹/₁₆ oz
Grip: Foamlite fore
Handle: Varmac, rubber butt cap, integral double-locking reel seat
Guides: Allan roller, roller top
Winding: Gudebrod size E; primary grey #602 double-wound; trim, black/white varigated #8002

B **30#:** Fenwick blank RT634; color, amber
Length: 5' 4", 1-piece blade
Weight: Blank, 6¼ oz; fitted, 12 oz
Grip: Foamlite fore
Handle: Allan #53308, gimbal butt, reel seat double-locking
Guides: AFTCO double roller lead, single roller running, roller top
Winding: Gudebrod size D; primary goldenrod #209 triple-wound; trim orange #221

(Text continued from page 153)

lengthwise strokes of the brush. And, to repeat something mentioned before, three or four thin coats, with ample drying time between them, are much better than two thick coats.

Always keep in mind when you're working on your RT rod blank that you must take special pains to leave no weak spots. If you do, a fish will find them. Then you'll be left, not with a smile on Candid Camera, but in a boat with a limp line and a sickly grin on your face, while the fish that might have gotten your name on the list of world record-holders goes back home to brag about the angler he got away from.

Glossary
of Rod Terms

Action: Relative distribution of flexibility and/or stiffness along a rod's length; or, manner in which a rod reacts to casting stress—thus, fast action, slow action, etc.

Baitcast rod: A short ($4^1/_2'$–6') rod designed for use with a revolving-spool reel; usually fitted with detachable grip.

Bamboo: also called cane. Also an abbreviated method of referring to a bamboo rod. May be described in terms of origin, Tonkin bamboo, Calcutta bamboo, etc.

Bay rod: A short ($5'$–$6^1/_2'$) rod used in saltwater fishing; also called boat rod, pier rod, or by other names applied to rods of this type.

Bent handle: Style of handle often fitted to saltwater trolling rods to give the angler improved leverage; has a bend or curve below the reel seat.

Bike rod: *see* Maxi-rod.

Blade: Working portion of any rod, the section above the grip.

Blank: A rod blade without fittings.

Boat rod: A short ($5'$–6') rod used in saltwater fishing.

Braced guides: Guides in which the foot arches up and is attached to the bottom rim of the ring.

Braced top: Tiptop with parallel braces extending from barrel to eye.

Bushing: Spacer of cork, wood, etc., between reel seat and blade designed to compensate for differences in diameter; reel seat is glued to bushing, which in turn is glued to butt of blade.

Butt: grip end of any rod.

Butt cap: Fitting used to close bottom of grip.

156

Butt ferrule: In baitcast and saltwater rods, a fitting used to adapt a rod's butt to the different diameter of its grip; in rods having more than two sections, the ferrule lowest on the blade.

Butt grip: Bottom portion of grip on rods in which grip is divided by reel seat.

Butt guide: Guide first above the grip; on fly rods, also called the stripping or stripper guide.

Butt joint: Lower section of a rod having two or more pieces.

Calcutta: Type of thick-walled bamboo, used unfitted as a pole.

Cane: Also called bamboo. Also, an unfitted or unworked stillfishing pole.

Carboloy: Trade name of a tungsten carbide alloy, used in guides.

Ceramic insert guides: Guides having an inner ring lined with a smooth, extremely hard ceramic material, usually aluminum oxide.

Chuck: Locking device used to secure rod blade to detachable handle.

Class, rod: Applied to rods meeting IGFA standards of specific action to line-test ratio; thus, such a rod would be described as being a "30-pound" or "40-pound," etc. class rod.

Collet: Clawlike fitting inside chuck of a detachable handle assembly, designed to grasp blade and hold it securely.

Color preservative: Acetone-based liquid applied to rod windings to prevent threads from turning dark when varnished.

Combination rod: Any rod intended to be used in more than one mode; often supplied with separate tips or grips.

Cork grip: Rod grip built up of layers of cork rings glued together, then filed and sanded to desired contour.

Detachable grip: Assembly used primarily with baitcast and saltwater rods, having integral reel seat and chuck or butt ferrule.

Double winding: A style of winding in which one course of thread is applied atop another. Used primarily in heavy-duty rods.

Fast action: Imprecise term susceptible to individual interpretation; generally applied to rods having light, responsive tips.

Fairy rod: Term applied to ultralight fly or spinning rod.

Feet, guide: Tapered metal extensions at right angles to ring over which thread is wound to secure guide to rod.

Female ferrule: Applied to open or socket half of a ferrule.

Ferrule: Friction device consisting of two metal tubes fitted one inside the other, used in joining rod sections temporarily.

Fiberglass, solid: Material used in making rod blades; consists of bundled glass filaments fused longitudinally into a cylinder by surrounding them with a flexible resin; the cylinder is then tapered on a centerless grinder.

Fiberglass, tubular: Material used in making rod blades; consists of longitudinal glass filaments wrapped in glass mesh, held around a tapered mandrel with flexible resin, cured by heat to form a light blade of predesigned weight and action.

Fittings: Components such as guides, reel seats, etc., used in making rods from blanks.

Flea rod: Ultralight rod. *See* Fairy rod; the terms are interchangeable, applied loosely and whimsically to rods of this type.

Fly rod: Rod of any length or material used in flycasting, distinguished by location of reel seat at bottom of grip.

Foregrip: Upper portion of grip on rods having grips divided by reel seat. *See* Butt grip.

Gathering guide: Butt guide, *which see.*

Gimbal: Metal cup inside a leather harness worn by saltwater anglers; by extension, the fitting on a rod butt that seats into the cup.

Glass: Abbreviated term applied to any fiberglass rod.

Glass-to-glass ferrules: Method of fitting a fiberglass rod with a short plug of solid fiberglass that extends beyond a section and mates with the inner wall of the jointing section.

Graphite: Carbonized fiber filaments fused together with elastic resin on mandrels to form rod blanks; also, generic term applied to all rods made from these blanks.

Grip: Portion of a rod held by the fisherman.

Grip check: Metal or plastic disk or cone fitted above a grip to conceal the gap between grip and blade. Also called winding check.

Guide: Loops or rings of varied sizes and materials through which line passes from reel to rod tip.

Handle: Wooden, cork, or metal detachable grip of saltwater rod.

Hood: Flared ring at one end of reel seat into which foot of reel fits; some reel seats have one fixed and one sliding hood, the latter being pushed into place with a locking ring.

Hook keeper: U-shaped fitting wound near the grip of a rod into which hook can be slipped when rod is not being used.

Hosel: Tapered cylinder 1 inch to as much as 3 inches long used to finish off and close either end of a grip.

Ice rod: Extremely short (10″–16″) rod used in fishing through ice. Also called a jig rod.

Impregnated rod: A bamboo rod made from strips into which a flexible resin has been infused by heat and/or pressure.

Jetty rod: Member of the boat/pier rod family, *which see.*

Jewelry: Trade term describing guides and other fittings.

Jig rod: Short rod used in jig-fishing; *see* Ice rod.

Joint: The point at which ferruled rod sections meet.

Keeper guides: Obsolete term; *see* Hook keeper.

Keeper rings: Wide rings fitted to slide along a grip and hold rod feet in position, in effect turning the grip into a reel seat.

Locking ring: Outer ring of a pair by which a reel-seat hood is adjusted; when tightened against the inner ring prevents this ring from working loose. Also, a ring on saltwater handles that locks the butt ferrule into the top of the handle.

Male ferrule: The half of a ferrule inserted into the socket when jointing a rod; also called the plug ferrule.

Micro-ferrule: A set or pair of ferrules shorter or lighter than conventional metal ferrules; also called mini-ferrules.

Maxi-rod: Unusually long (12′–16′) and whippy rod designed to be used with monofil in the 2#–4# test range; also called bike rod.

Modulus: Inherent flexibility of any material, its capacity to bend under stress before breaking; thus, a high-modulus material has greater strength in ratio to bulk than a low-modulus material, while a low-modulus material will form a more pronounced arc before breaking.

Muskie rod: An extra-stout baitcasting-type rod with long grips, fitted with a trigger reel seat; indigenous to the Upper Midwestern U. S. and Canada. See Popping rod.

Neutral axis: The area of a rod where arc of tip and stiffness of butt come together; thus, the portion of a rod that does no work.

Offset grip: A grip at an angle to the longitudinal plane of a rod, generally fitted on baitcast rods; offset grips usually have integral reel seats.

Offset reel seat: Reel seat below the longitudinal axis of the rod and grip.

Overwinding: *see* Double winding.

Pack rod: A rod in shorter than normal sections designed for easy portability.

Parabolic: A blade that flexes equally through its entire length when under stress, forming a parabola.

Pear tip: Type of tiptop fitted to fly rods, an oval-shaped loop blunt at the top and tapering to a point at the barrel.

Pier rod: *see* Boat rod.

Plug: In rod parlance, a short, tapered cylinder inserted to reinforce the walls of a tubular fiberglass rod at ferrule and butt points.

Plug ferrule: *see* Male ferrule.

Pole: Any type of fishing rod without fittings.

Popping rod: A type of long ($5^1/_2'$–$7'$) rod with stiff tip and trigger reel seat used in fresh and salt water with popping lures.

Power axis: Center point of the arc formed by a rod flexed under stress; thus, the area doing the most work.

RT rod: Regulation Tackle rod, a saltwater trolling rod meeting IGFA standards; also referred to by class, as a 30- or 40-pound class rod.

Reel seat: Metal cylinder, one end externally threaded and fitted with a threaded ring, the other end fitted with a hood. The reel is locked firmly in position by the pressure of the ring on the reel's feet. *See* Keeper rings.

Ring guide: Guide in which ring or eye is attached to sidepieces arching up from the feet; see Braced guides. Also called rigid guides to distinguish them from the obsolete ring-and-keeper guides used on early rods.

Roller guide: Guide equipped with grooved rollers rather than rings or loops. The rollers are held on axles supported by the sidepieces, and may be equipped with ball bearings; the line passes over the rollers. Used on saltwater rods, especially when metal lines are employed.

Roller top: Also called roller tiptop. Rod top made like roller guides.

Salmon fly rod: a long ($10'$–$14'$) fly rod with a two-hand grip.

Section: any piece of a jointed rod; thus, a two-piece rod will have two sections, butt and tip; a three-piece rod will have butt, middle, and tip sections.

Set: Curve formed in a rod by stress, age, or improper storage.

Socket ferrule: *see* Female ferrule.

Snake guide: One-piece humped guide formed from wire into an open arc, used on fly rods.

Spincast rod: A medium ($5'$–$6^1/_2'$) length rod designed for use with closed-face spinning reels.

Spine: Longitudinal plane of a tubular fiberglass rod blank along which the mesh was overlapped during manufacture, The spine and the plane

180° opposed to it are the "strong" sides of such a blank. Often confused with Spline, *which see.*

Spinning rod: Light, medium to long (5$^1/_2$'–9') rod designed to be used with open-faced spinning reels.

Spinning rod guide: Also called spinning guide; a ring guide having large rings of thin metal designed for use on spinning rods.

Spline: One of the strips glued together to make a bamboo rod; in the most common construction, six splines shaved to a taper at a 60° angle are glued together to form a blade hexagonal in cross-section.

Surf rod: A long (9'–14') heavy-duty rod designed for long casts from shore; may be fitted for use with revolving spool or spinning reels.

Taper: The swelling of a blade from tip to butt, which may be even or modified in certain areas; blades so modified are described as having "fast tip" or other types of action.

Telescoping pole: Tubular fiberglass pole with nesting sections that when extended make a stillfishing pole 10'–16' long. Also called a Whipout.

Threads: The thread used in winding a rod.

Tip: Upper section of a jointed rod, or the top 3 to 6 inches of any rod.

Tonkin: A variety of bamboo preferred by rod makers.

Travel rod: *see* Pack rod.

Triple winding: A winding consisting of three courses of thread, one atop the other, used on heavy-duty rods.

Tungsten carbide: An alloy of tungsten steel and carbide used in making ring guides and tiptops.

Underwinding: Bottom course of a double or triple winding.

Unlimited rod: Saltwater trolling rod not meeting IGFA standards, usually of heavier construction than the RT 130-pound rod.

Varnish: In contemporary usage, any varnish-type preparation used as a protective coating over rod windings.

Wall: Qualified by "thin" or "thick" to describe the two most common types of tubular fiberglass blade.

Whipout: *see* Telescoping pole.

Winding: Closely spaced turns of thread used in fitting guides to a blade; or any decorative thread wrapped on a rod.

Wrapping: Often used interchangeably with winding.

Manufacturers and Suppliers

Please remember that not all the firms listed here sell direct to consumers. All or most of the manufacturers will provide you with the names and addresses of dealers in your area, however. Most of them will send you a catalog. In the case of retailers and mail-order houses, I've done business with most of those listed, often on a test basis, and have listed no retail suppliers whose service I've found unsatisfactory.

Allan Tackle Manufacturing Co.
325 Duffy Avenue
Hicksville, NY 11801
> Manufacturer of guides, reel seats, ferrules, other fittings. No retail sales from factory but will supply names and addresses of local dealers. Catalog.

Angler's Pro Shop
Box 35
Springfield, OH 45501
> Retail mail-order supplier of rod-building parts, fiberglass and graphite blanks, kits. Catalog.

Axelson Fishing Tackle Mfg. Co.
1559 Placentia Ave.
Newport Beach, CA 92663
> Manufacturer of AFTCO roller guides and roller tops, aluminum saltwater rod handles, other fittings. Catalog.

Brookstone Company
12 Brookstone Building
Peterborough, NH 03458
> Retail mail-order supplier of specialty woodworking and metalworking tools. Catalog.

Cabela's
812 Thirteenth Ave.
Sidney, NE 69162
Retail mail-order supplier of graphite and fiberglass blanks, kits, rod-building materials. Catalog.

Childre, Lew & Sons
Box 535
Foley, AL 36535
Manufacturers and importers of Fuji guides, graphite and fiberglass blanks, fittings. No retail sales from factory. Catalog.

California Tackle Co.
430 West Redondo Beach Blvd.
Gardena, CA 90248
Manufacturer of Sabre fiberglass rod blanks, saltwater handles. No retail sales from factory. Catalog.

Dale Clemens Custom Tackle
Route 2, Box 850C
Wescosville, PA 18106
Custom rod maker, mail-order supplier of rod-building components. Catalog.

Featherweight Products
3454 Ocean View Blvd.
Glendale, CA 91208
Manufacturer and mail-order supplier of Rawhide fiberglass and graphite blanks, Sizmatic ferrules, Foamlite and Hypalon grips, other rod-making materials. Rod-making brochure. Catalog.

Fenwick
14799 Chestnut St.
Box 729
Westminster, CA 92683
Manufacturer of HMG Graphite, Fenglas, and Feralite blanks, baitcast rod handles, saltwater handles. No retail sales from factory; will provide addresses of local dealers. Rod-making brochure. Catalog.

Finnysports
2910 Glanzman Rd.
Toledo, OH 43614
Retail mail-order supplier of graphite and fiberglass blanks, kits, rod-making materials. Catalog.

Fly Line
2935 Washington Blvd.
Ogden, UT 84401
Retail mail-order supplier of rod-building components.

Gudebrod Bros. Silk Co.
12 South 12th Street
Philadelphia, PA 19107
Manufacturers of rod-winding silk and nylon threads, Butt Wind, Aetna Foulproof guides, finishes, adhesives. No retail sales from factory. Rod-winding brochure. Catalog.

Herter's, Inc.
Waseca, MN 56093
Retail mail-order supplier of fiberglass blanks, kits, rod-making materials. Catalog.

E. Hille
815 Railway St.
Williamsport, PA 17701
Retail mail-order supplier of fiberglass and graphite blanks, kits, rod-making materials. Catalog.

J. Kennedy Fisher, Inc.
6701 11th Avenue
Los Angeles, CA 90043
Manufacturer and mail-order supplier of graphite and fiberglass blanks and kits. Catalog.

Kodiak Corp.
Box 467
Ironwood, MI 49938
Manufacturer of fiberglass and solid glass rod blanks. No retail sales from factory. Catalog.

Lamiglas, Inc.
Box 148
Woodland, WA 98674
Manufacturer of graphite and fiberglass blanks. No retail sales from factory but will supply dealer information. Catalog.

Midland Tackle Co.
66 Route 17
Sloatsburg, NY 10974
Retail mail-order supplier of fiberglass, graphite, and, in limited quantities, bamboo blanks, kits, rod-building materials. Catalog.

Mildrum Manufacturing Co.
230 Berlin St.
East Berlin, CT 06023
Manufacturer of freshwater guides and saltwater roller guides and tops. No retail sales from factory. Catalog.

Netcraft Co.
3101 Sylvania St.
Toledo, OH 43613
Retail mail-order supplier of fiberglass blanks, kits, rod-making supplies.
Catalog.

Orvis Company
Manchester, VT 05254
Manufacturer and mail-order supplier of bamboo, graphite and fi-
berglass kits, rod-making materials. Catalog.

Plas/Steel Products, Inc.
Walkerton, IN 46574
Manufacturer of solid glass blanks. No retail sales.

Reed Tackle Co.
Box 390
Caldwell, NJ 07006
Retail mail-order supplier of fiberglass blanks, kits, rod-making materi-
als. Catalog.

Reinke Brothers
3144 West Greenfield Ave.
Milwaukee, WI 53215
Retail mail-order suppliers of graphite and fiberglass blanks, kits, rod-
making supplies. Catalog.

Rod & Reel
Box 132D
Leola, PA 17540
Manufacturer and mail-order supplier of impregnated bamboo blanks
and rod-building components. Catalog.

Rodmaker's Supply
1408 Palmer Ave.
Muskegon, MI 49441
Retail mail-order supplier of graphite and fiberglass blanks, kits, rod-
making materials. Catalog.

Scientific Anglers
Box 2001
Midland, MI 48640
Manufacturer of graphite fly rod blanks. Retail sales from factory only to
areas lacking local dealers. Will supply dealer information. Catalog.

Scott Powr-ply Co.
111 Cook Street
San Francisco, CA 94118
Manufacturer and mail-order supplier of graphite and fiberglass blanks.

Shakespeare Company
Box 246
Columbia, SC 29202
> Manufacturer of graphite and Howald process fiberglass blanks. No retail sales from factory. Catalog.

Shoff's Sporting Goods
406 West Meeker St.
Kent, WA 98031
> Retail mail-order supplier of graphite and fiberglass blanks, kits, rodmaking supplies. Catalog.

St. Croix Corp.
9909 South Shore Dr.
Minneapolis, MN 55441
> Manufacturer of fiberglass blanks. No retail sales from factory. Catalog.

Tackle Shop
Limit Manufacturing Co.
Box 369
106 Arapaho Central Park
Richardson, TX 75080
> Retail mail-order supplier of graphite and fiberglass blanks, rod-making materials. Catalog.

Varmac Manufacturing Co.
4201 Redwood Ave.
Los Angeles, CA 90066
> Manufacturer of guides, reel seats, handles, other rod-making materials. No retail sales from factory. Catalog.

Walton Powell
1148 West 8th Avenue
Chico, CA 95926
> Manufacturer of bamboo rods, graphite and fiberglass rods and blanks (no bamboo blanks). Mail-order supplier of blanks.

R. L. Winston Rod Co.
Box 248
Twin Bridges, MT 59754
> Manufacturer and mail-order supplier of custom rods, bamboo, graphite and fiberglass blanks, and components. Catalog.

Index